True Stories of Prison Escapes

Shah Rukh

Published by Shah Rukh, 2024.

While every precaution has been taken in the preparation of this book, the publisher assumes no responsibility for errors or omissions, or for damages resulting from the use of the information contained herein.

TRUE STORIES OF PRISON ESCAPES

First edition. May 21, 2024.

ISBN: 979-8224333332

Written by Shah Rukh.

Table of Contents

Prologue

In the annals of human history, few tales captivate the imagination and stir the soul quite like those of daring prison escapes. From the confines of concrete walls to the vast expanse of the open world, these stories of resilience, ingenuity, and defiance against the odds have etched themselves into the fabric of our collective consciousness.

In the shadows of society's darkest corners, where the clang of iron bars and the echo of footsteps on cold, stone floors are a constant reminder of captivity, individuals have dared to dream of freedom. Through cunning, courage, and sheer determination, they have defied the shackles of incarceration and embarked on perilous journeys to reclaim their liberty.

"True Stories of Prison Escapes" is a chronicle of these remarkable feats of human endeavor, each chapter a testament to the indomitable spirit of those who refuse to be confined by the constraints of their circumstances. From the infamous Alcatraz Escape to the audacious breakout from Shawshank State Penitentiary, these tales offer a glimpse into the hearts and minds of those who have dared to defy authority and embrace the pursuit of freedom at any cost.

As we embark on this journey through the annals of history, let us bear witness to the triumphs and tragedies, the victories and defeats, of those who have dared to challenge the boundaries of human endurance and rewrite the narrative of their own lives. For in the stories of these brave souls, we find echoes of our own struggles, our own hopes, and our own aspirations for a life lived free from the constraints of captivity.

So join me, dear reader, as we embark on a journey through the labyrinthine corridors of prisons and the vast expanses of the open world, guided by the flickering light of hope and the unwavering resolve of those who refuse to be bound by the chains of fate. For in their stories, we find not only tales of escape, but also lessons of resilience, courage, and the unyielding power of the human spirit.

Chapter 1: Frank Abagnale Jr

Frank William Abagnale Jr. is one of the most notorious and intriguing figures in the history of crime, particularly known for his audacious escapes, brilliant cons, and incredible ability to assume multiple identities. His life story, as dramatized in the 2002 movie *Catch Me If You Can*, has fascinated millions, but the real-life escapades of Frank Abagnale Jr. are even more astonishing than Hollywood could portray.

Early Life and the Seed of Deception

Born on April 27, 1948, in Bronxville, New York, Frank Abagnale Jr. was the third of four children. His father, Frank Abagnale Sr., was a successful business owner, while his mother, Paulette, was a French-American who met Frank Sr. during World War II. The family was financially well-off, but turmoil brewed beneath the surface. When Abagnale was 16, his parents divorced, a life-changing event that deeply affected him. This period of instability, coupled with his teenage rebellion, marked the beginning of his foray into a life of crime.

Initially, Abagnale's cons were small-scale. He began by committing petty crimes such as stealing gasoline and writing bad checks. His early attempts at deception were crude, but his natural intelligence and charm allowed him to refine his methods quickly. By the time he left home at 16, Abagnale was ready to take on bigger and bolder schemes.

The Impersonations Begin: Pilot, Doctor, Lawyer

Abagnale's most famous exploits revolve around his ability to impersonate professionals, a skill he developed with remarkable ease and success. His first major con was perhaps his most famous: impersonating a Pan American World Airways pilot. Abagnale was inspired by his fascination with airplanes and the prestige that came with being a pilot. At the age of 18, using a fake ID and a doctored pilot's license, he successfully convinced Pan Am officials that he was a pilot.

This audacious deception allowed Abagnale to travel over 1,000,000 miles on over 250 flights to 26 countries, all without ever flying a plane. His impersonation was so convincing that he was often invited to sit in the cockpit during flights. The "deadheading" scheme—where airline employees hitch rides on other flights for free—enabled him to travel across the globe, stay in luxurious hotels, and enjoy fine dining, all at the airline's expense. Remarkably, during this time, he never piloted an aircraft, instead charming his way through security and gaining access to flights without any suspicion.

After his success as a fake pilot, Abagnale turned to other professions. He impersonated a doctor at a Georgia hospital for nearly a year. Without any medical training, Abagnale was able to supervise interns, write prescriptions, and even assist in minor procedures. He took on the role of a chief resident pediatrician at the Cobb General Hospital by forging his credentials. The fact that he was able to pull this off without causing any harm to patients is nothing short of miraculous. His natural charisma and quick thinking allowed him to avoid situations where his lack of medical knowledge would be exposed.

Abagnale didn't stop there. He also assumed the identity of a lawyer. With a forged Harvard Law transcript, he applied for a position as an assistant attorney general in Louisiana. Despite never attending law school, Abagnale passed the Louisiana Bar Exam after two failed attempts, a testament to his intellect and ability to study under pressure. He worked in this role for eight months before moving on to his next con.

The Art of Check Forgery

While his impersonations were spectacular, it was Abagnale's expertise in check forgery that truly set him apart as a criminal mastermind. Between the ages of 16 and 21, Abagnale defrauded banks out of $2.5 million through an elaborate series of check schemes. He was so proficient at this that the FBI later recruited him to help them understand and combat check fraud.

Abagnale's schemes were multifaceted. He would often create fraudulent checks using sophisticated techniques that were nearly impossible to detect at the time. In one instance, he discovered that by depositing a personal check into his account and then withdrawing money before the check cleared, he could effectively float funds between accounts. He also employed a method known as "paperhanging," where he would write checks on overdrawn accounts. Abagnale even printed his own checks, mimicking the designs of legitimate companies, which he then cashed at banks across the country.

He was known to use various methods to pass bad checks, including altering bank account numbers on deposit slips so that the money from legitimate deposits went into his account instead of the intended recipient's. This technique allowed him to amass large sums of money quickly. Abagnale's understanding of the banking system and his ability to exploit its weaknesses made him one of the most successful check forgers in history.

Escapes and Run-Ins with the Law

Despite his extraordinary success as a con artist, Abagnale's luck eventually ran out. His first major arrest occurred in 1969 in Montpellier, France, after an Air France flight attendant recognized him from a wanted poster. His international crimes caught up with him, and he was jailed in Perpignan, France. The French prison system was notoriously harsh, and Abagnale was placed in a cell that was so small he could barely lie down. He spent six months there under brutal conditions before being extradited to Sweden to face charges of forgery.

In Sweden, Abagnale was treated more humanely, but his crimes there led to a sentence that would see him extradited to the United States. However, before his return to the U.S., he was allowed to remain in Sweden for a short period, during which he discovered a legal loophole. His extradition papers were not properly processed, and as a result, the Swedish government granted him temporary asylum. This was a brief reprieve, as Sweden eventually deported him back to the U.S.

Back in the United States, Abagnale faced the full wrath of the law. He was sentenced to 12 years in prison at the Federal Correctional Institution in Petersburg, Virginia. However, Frank Abagnale Jr. wasn't about to give up his freedom so easily. He managed to escape from custody not once, but twice, during his imprisonment.

His first escape attempt was nothing short of brilliant. While being transported to a federal prison, Abagnale was able to convince the guards that he was actually an undercover prison inspector. He had noticed that actual prison inspectors were treated with a higher level of respect and had more privileges. By exploiting this knowledge, he persuaded the guards to remove his handcuffs and take him to a more comfortable holding area. From there, he managed to slip away, temporarily regaining his freedom.

Abagnale's second escape was even more audacious. While at the Federal Detention Center in Atlanta, he posed as an undercover prison inspector yet again. This time, he convinced a prison guard to help him escape by claiming that he was working on a secret operation to expose corruption within the prison. The guard, believing Abagnale's story, arranged for him to be escorted out of the facility. Once outside, Abagnale disappeared into the night.

Unfortunately for Abagnale, his freedom was short-lived. He was recaptured after a few weeks and returned to prison. Despite these escapes, his charm and wit earned him the attention of the FBI, who eventually offered him a deal: in exchange for his freedom, he would help the Bureau combat fraud and catch other criminals like himself.

Redemption and a New Life

After serving just five years of his 12-year sentence, Abagnale was released on the condition that he would assist the FBI in investigating fraud and teaching law enforcement how to identify and stop scams. He accepted the offer and spent the next several decades working as a consultant for the government and private companies.

In 1976, Abagnale established his own consultancy firm, Abagnale & Associates, which specializes in fraud prevention and cybersecurity. His unique insight into the criminal mind and his expertise in the areas of forgery and deception have made him a highly sought-after speaker and consultant. Abagnale has since worked with hundreds of institutions, including major corporations, law enforcement agencies, and government bodies, to help them secure their systems against fraud.

He also authored a number of books, including his autobiography *Catch Me If You Can*, which was adapted into the aforementioned film starring Leonardo DiCaprio and Tom Hanks. The success of the movie brought Abagnale's story to a new generation, cementing his place as one of the most infamous and fascinating criminals of the 20th century.

Legacy and Reflection

Today, Frank Abagnale Jr. is seen not only as a criminal mastermind but also as a reformed man who has used his talents for the greater good. His story is one of transformation, where a teenage con artist evolved into a respected authority on fraud prevention. Abagnale's life serves as a reminder of the thin line between genius and criminality and how one's skills can be used for both harm and good.

Abagnale himself has expressed remorse for his actions, often reflecting on the impact his crimes had on his victims. He has stated in interviews that he regrets the choices he made in his youth and is grateful for the opportunity to make amends through his work. His life story continues to be a source of fascination, not just for its audacity and brilliance, but for the remarkable turnaround that followed.

In the annals of crime history, Frank Abagnale Jr. stands out as a figure of both infamy and redemption, a man who mastered the art of deception, but ultimately found a way to use his knowledge to help others. His journey from con artist to crime consultant is a testament to the complexity of human nature and the possibility of change, even for those who have walked a dark path.

Chapter 2: John Dillinger

John Dillinger, often referred to as America's most notorious bank robber, became a symbol of the public's fascination with outlaws during the Great Depression. His criminal career, marked by daring heists, dramatic escapes, and a relentless pursuit by law enforcement, has left an indelible mark on American history. Dillinger's life story is a complex narrative of crime, celebrity, and the intense efforts to bring him to justice.

Early Life and the Seeds of Crime

John Herbert Dillinger was born on June 22, 1903, in Indianapolis, Indiana, to a working-class family. His father, John Wilson Dillinger, was a strict and often harsh man, while his mother, Mary Ellen Lancaster, passed away when John was just three years old. This loss deeply affected young Dillinger, leading to a troubled childhood. His father remarried, but Dillinger struggled to adjust to the new family dynamic, often finding himself in conflict with his stepmother and father.

Dillinger's early years were marked by a growing sense of rebellion. He was known as a troublemaker in school, frequently skipping classes and getting into fights. At the age of 16, he dropped out of school and began working at a machine shop. However, the monotony of factory work did little to curb his restlessness. Dillinger soon fell in with a group of petty criminals, and his descent into a life of crime began.

In 1924, at the age of 21, Dillinger committed his first major crime. Along with a friend, he attempted to rob a local grocer named Frank Morgan. The robbery was poorly planned and quickly went awry. Dillinger was caught and, under the advice of his father, pleaded guilty, hoping for leniency. Instead, he was sentenced to 10 to 20 years in prison. This harsh sentence would prove to be a turning point in Dillinger's life, solidifying his commitment to a life of crime.

The Birth of a Criminal Mastermind in Prison

Dillinger's time in prison was transformative. Rather than being rehabilitated, he used his incarceration to learn the finer points of criminal activity. He became close with a group of seasoned bank robbers, including Harry "Pete" Pierpont, Charles Makley, and Homer Van Meter. These men were experienced criminals who taught Dillinger the skills he would later use in his own bank-robbing career. They discussed strategies for robbing banks, escaping from prisons, and avoiding law enforcement.

Dillinger quickly earned a reputation as a charismatic and intelligent inmate. He studied every aspect of bank robbery, from the layout of vaults to the operation of alarm systems. His fellow inmates recognized his potential, and they began to plan a series of heists they would execute once they were released. Dillinger also kept himself physically fit, often exercising in his cell to maintain his strength and agility.

In May 1933, after serving nearly nine years, Dillinger was paroled. His time in prison had hardened him, and he emerged as a determined and ruthless criminal. Upon his release, he immediately began to assemble a gang with the intention of carrying out a series of high-profile bank robberies.

The Rise of Public Enemy Number One

Dillinger wasted no time putting his newfound knowledge to use. In June 1933, just a month after his release, he and his gang carried out their first bank robbery in New Carlisle, Ohio, making off with $10,000. The heist was a success, and it marked the beginning of Dillinger's infamous crime spree. Over the next year, Dillinger and his gang would rob more than a dozen banks across the Midwest, amassing a fortune in stolen cash and becoming the FBI's top priority.

What set Dillinger apart from other criminals of his time was his daring and audacity. He and his gang often robbed banks in broad daylight, using military-style tactics to overwhelm bank employees and law enforcement. Dillinger's meticulous planning ensured that these heists were executed with precision and efficiency. His gang would often hold hostages as human shields, preventing police from opening fire as they made their escape.

Dillinger's ability to outsmart the authorities only added to his legend. He was known for his quick getaways, often using stolen cars to flee the scene of a crime. His gang became experts at avoiding police roadblocks and even engaged in shootouts with law enforcement on several occasions. Despite the violence associated with his crimes, Dillinger's charm and good looks made him a folk hero to many Americans struggling during the Great Depression. He was seen as a Robin Hood-like figure, taking from the rich banks that were blamed for the economic hardships of the time.

Escapes from Justice

Dillinger's criminal career was punctuated by a series of daring escapes that only added to his notoriety. His first major escape came in September 1933, just a few months after his initial bank robberies. Dillinger was arrested in Dayton, Ohio, after being caught with a cache of weapons and stolen goods. He was taken to the county jail in Lima, Ohio, to await trial. However, Dillinger's gang had no intention of letting him stay behind bars.

On October 12, 1933, just weeks after his arrest, three members of Dillinger's gang arrived at the Lima jail, posing as Indiana State Police officers. They claimed they were there to extradite Dillinger to Indiana for questioning. The ruse worked, and the jail's sheriff, Jesse Sarber, asked to see their credentials. When he turned his back, one of the gang members pulled out a gun and shot Sarber dead. The gang then freed Dillinger from his cell and fled, leaving behind a trail of chaos and a dead sheriff.

This escape was a turning point in Dillinger's criminal career. It demonstrated not only his cunning but also his willingness to use violence to achieve his goals. The escape also marked the beginning of a relentless manhunt by the FBI, which had recently been granted the authority to pursue criminals across state lines.

Dillinger's most famous escape occurred on March 3, 1934, from the Lake County Jail in Crown Point, Indiana. He had been captured in Tucson, Arizona, in January of that year, after a fire in a hotel led police to discover his hideout. Dillinger was extradited to Indiana to stand trial for the murder of an East Chicago police officer during a bank robbery. The Crown Point jail was considered escape-proof, and Dillinger was kept under heavy guard.

However, Dillinger had other plans. On the morning of March 3, he managed to obtain a fake gun, which he used to intimidate the guards. Some accounts suggest that the gun was carved from wood and painted black, while others claim it was a real weapon smuggled in by an accomplice. Regardless of its origin, Dillinger's bluff worked. He forced the guards to open his cell and locked them inside. He then walked out of the jail and stole the sheriff's car, making his escape.

This brazen escape further humiliated law enforcement and cemented Dillinger's status as Public Enemy Number One. The FBI, under the leadership of J. Edgar Hoover, intensified its efforts to capture Dillinger, viewing his arrest as a matter of national importance. The escape also led to a nationwide media frenzy, with newspapers and radio stations covering every detail of Dillinger's exploits.

The Downfall of a Legend

Despite his success as a criminal, Dillinger's luck began to run out in the spring of 1934. The FBI was closing in, and several members of his gang were either captured or killed in shootouts with law enforcement. Dillinger himself was almost caught in April 1934 during a raid on an apartment in St. Paul, Minnesota. He managed to escape, but was shot in the leg during the confrontation.

Desperate and on the run, Dillinger underwent plastic surgery in May 1934 to alter his appearance and remove his fingerprints. The surgery was performed by an underworld doctor, and while it was somewhat successful in changing Dillinger's looks, it left him with visible scars. Dillinger also adopted a new alias, going by the name of Jimmy Lawrence.

Despite these efforts to evade capture, Dillinger's days were numbered. He continued to rob banks, but the pressure from law enforcement was relentless. The FBI had expanded its network of informants and was using new forensic techniques to track Dillinger's movements. The public's fascination with Dillinger also meant that he could not go anywhere without being recognized.

The end came on July 22, 1934, in Chicago. Dillinger was betrayed by a woman named Anna Sage, a Romanian immigrant who operated a brothel in the city. Sage, who was facing deportation, made a deal with the FBI to turn Dillinger in, in exchange for leniency in her immigration case. She arranged to meet Dillinger at the Biograph Theater, where they planned to see the movie *Manhattan Melodrama*.

That evening, Dillinger, Sage, and another woman named Polly Hamilton went to the theater. Unbeknownst to Dillinger, the FBI had surrounded the area, waiting for him to emerge. Sage had signaled

Dillinger's presence by wearing an orange dress, which later became known as the "Lady in Red" dress, although it was actually orange.

As Dillinger left the theater, FBI agents moved in. He realized too late that he had been betrayed and attempted to flee down an alley. Agents fired several shots, hitting Dillinger three times. He collapsed and died at the scene. The public, which had followed Dillinger's exploits with a mixture of awe and fear, was both shocked and fascinated by his death. His body was put on display at the Cook County Morgue, where thousands of people came to see the fallen outlaw.

Legacy and Cultural Impact

John Dillinger's life and death left an enduring legacy in American culture. During his criminal career, he became a symbol of defiance against authority, particularly during a time when many Americans felt oppressed by the economic hardships of the Great Depression. His daring bank robberies and escapes captivated the public's imagination, and he was often depicted as a modern-day Robin Hood, even though there is little evidence to suggest that he shared his ill-gotten gains with the poor.

Dillinger's story has been the subject of numerous books, movies, and television shows. Perhaps the most famous portrayal of Dillinger came in the 2009 film *Public Enemies*, in which Johnny Depp played the role of Dillinger. The film highlighted the cat-and-mouse game between Dillinger and the FBI, as well as the outlaw's larger-than-life persona.

Dillinger's life also contributed to significant changes in law enforcement. His ability to evade capture for so long led to the expansion of the FBI's powers, including the authority to carry firearms and make arrests. The agency's use of scientific methods, such as fingerprint analysis and ballistics, also became more prominent in the hunt for Dillinger. His death marked the beginning of the end of the

"Public Enemy" era, as many of his contemporaries were either captured or killed in the following months.

In the years since his death, Dillinger has continued to be a subject of fascination and controversy. His grave in Crown Hill Cemetery in Indianapolis has been visited by thousands of people, some of whom leave coins, flowers, and other mementos. There have also been persistent rumors and conspiracy theories suggesting that Dillinger faked his death and lived out the rest of his life under an assumed identity, though these claims have never been substantiated.

Ultimately, John Dillinger's story is one of a man who became larger than life, both in his own time and in the decades that followed. His rise from a troubled youth to America's most wanted criminal, his audacious escapes, and his eventual downfall have all contributed to his enduring status as one of the most iconic figures in American criminal history. While his actions were undoubtedly criminal, the legend of John Dillinger continues to captivate the imagination, reflecting the complex relationship between society and those who live outside the law.

Chapter 3: Alcatraz Escape

The Alcatraz escape of June 11, 1962, is one of the most famous and intriguing prison break stories in American history. The daring escape from Alcatraz Federal Penitentiary, also known as "The Rock," captivated the nation and left law enforcement puzzled. It involved three men—Frank Morris and brothers John and Clarence Anglin—who ingeniously devised and executed a plan to escape from what was considered one of the most secure prisons in the world. To this day, the fate of the escapees remains unknown, and the event has become a subject of endless speculation, myth, and legend.

Alcatraz: The Inescapable Fortress

Alcatraz Federal Penitentiary, located on Alcatraz Island in San Francisco Bay, was established in 1934 as a maximum-security facility designed to house the most dangerous criminals in the United States. The island's natural defenses—cold, treacherous waters, strong currents, and the sheer distance from the mainland—made it an ideal location for a prison intended to be inescapable.

Alcatraz housed some of the most notorious criminals of the era, including Al Capone, George "Machine Gun" Kelly, and Robert Stroud, the "Birdman of Alcatraz." The prison's reputation as an impregnable fortress was bolstered by its strict security measures, including constant surveillance, regular headcounts, and reinforced cells. The walls were thick, the bars were steel, and the guards were vigilant. Escape attempts were considered suicidal, and any attempt to flee the island was met with swift and often lethal force.

Despite its formidable defenses, Alcatraz was not without its weaknesses. The prison was old, and its infrastructure was beginning to show signs of wear and tear. Over time, the inmates, many of whom were intelligent and resourceful, began to identify and exploit these vulnerabilities. This is precisely what Frank Morris and the Anglin brothers did, turning the seemingly impossible task of escaping from Alcatraz into a meticulously planned operation.

The Masterminds: Frank Morris and the Anglin Brothers

Frank Lee Morris, born in Washington, D.C., in 1926, was the mastermind behind the escape. Morris had a long history of criminal activity, including armed robbery and burglary, and had escaped from several prisons before being sent to Alcatraz in 1960. Morris was highly intelligent, with an IQ of 133, and was known for his cunning and resourcefulness. His ability to outthink authorities had earned him a reputation as a skilled escape artist.

The Anglin brothers, John William Anglin and Clarence Anglin, were born into a poor farming family in Donalsonville, Georgia. They had a history of bank robbery, which led to their incarceration in various prisons before being transferred to Alcatraz. The brothers were close, having grown up working together and committing crimes together. Their bond and mutual trust made them ideal partners in the escape plot.

The trio met at Alcatraz, where they were all housed in adjacent cells in Block B. Over time, they began to discuss the possibility of escape. They were later joined by a fourth conspirator, Allen West, who occupied a cell near Morris and the Anglins. Together, they began to develop an elaborate plan to escape from Alcatraz.

The Escape Plan: Ingenuity and Determination

The escape plan was a product of meticulous planning, patience, and sheer ingenuity. The men spent months preparing for their escape, carefully crafting tools and devising a strategy that would take advantage of the prison's weaknesses.

The first step in the plan involved creating a way to access the utility corridor located behind their cells. Each of the conspirators used crude tools, including spoons, metal strips, and an electric drill fashioned from a vacuum cleaner motor, to slowly enlarge the ventilation ducts in their cells. The men worked at night, carefully removing the grates and chipping away at the concrete walls surrounding the ducts. To avoid detection, they concealed their work using painted cardboard replicas of the vents.

Once they had created openings large enough to pass through, the men entered the utility corridor, which was unguarded and provided access to the prison's roof. They took turns working on their escape, and after several months, they had successfully opened the ducts in all four cells.

The next phase of the plan involved creating a means of escape from the island itself. The men knew that the cold, choppy waters of San Francisco Bay were their biggest obstacle. To overcome this, they constructed makeshift life vests and a raft from raincoats that they had stolen or scavenged over time. They used more than 50 raincoats, which were stitched together and sealed with heat from nearby steam pipes. The raft, once inflated, would be their ticket to freedom.

In addition to the raft, the men created dummy heads made from a mixture of soap, concrete dust, and toilet paper. These heads were meticulously painted and adorned with hair collected from the prison's barbershop. The purpose of the dummy heads was to fool the guards during nighttime bed checks, giving the escapees enough time to make their getaway before their absence was noticed.

The Escape: A Night of Boldness and Desperation

On the night of June 11, 1962, the escape plan was put into action. Morris, the Anglin brothers, and West made their final preparations and waited for the cover of darkness. West, however, encountered a problem: the hole he had created in his cell wall was too small, and he was unable to squeeze through it. As a result, he was left behind, while the other three men proceeded with the escape.

Morris and the Anglins climbed through their enlarged ventilation ducts into the utility corridor and made their way to the roof. From there, they climbed down a 50-foot pipe to the ground below. They then made their way to the northeastern shore of the island, where they inflated their makeshift raft using a concertina, a type of musical instrument that could be used as a bellows.

The three men launched their raft into the cold waters of San Francisco Bay, aiming to reach the mainland or the nearby Angel Island. The strong currents, cold water, and the darkness of the night made the journey perilous. The men were last seen by the other inmates as they disappeared into the night, leaving behind a prison that had once been considered inescapable.

The Aftermath: An Enduring Mystery

The morning after the escape, guards discovered the dummy heads in the escapees' beds and quickly realized that a breakout had occurred. A massive manhunt was launched, involving law enforcement agencies across the country. The FBI, the U.S. Coast Guard, and local police scoured the bay and the surrounding areas, searching for any sign of the escapees.

Despite their efforts, no definitive evidence of the men's fate was ever found. A few days after the escape, a paddle, some personal belongings, and pieces of the raft were discovered floating in the bay, leading authorities to believe that the men had drowned. The official conclusion by the FBI was that the escapees likely perished in the treacherous waters, but the lack of bodies or conclusive evidence left the case open to speculation.

Over the years, there have been numerous reported sightings of the escapees, as well as claims that they had successfully made it to freedom and were living under assumed identities. The Anglin family, in particular, has maintained that John and Clarence survived the escape and made contact with them in the years that followed. They presented evidence, including Christmas cards and photographs, that they claimed were sent by the brothers after their escape.

In 1979, the FBI officially closed the case, citing a lack of credible leads. However, in 2013, a letter allegedly written by John Anglin surfaced, claiming that he and his brother had survived the escape and were living in secret. The letter, which was sent to the San Francisco Police Department, reignited interest in the case, but its authenticity has never been confirmed.

The mystery of the Alcatraz escape continues to captivate the public imagination. The idea that three men could have outwitted the authorities, survived the treacherous waters of San Francisco Bay, and vanished without a trace is both thrilling and tantalizing. The escape has been the subject of countless books, documentaries, and films, most notably the 1979 movie *Escape from Alcatraz*, starring Clint Eastwood as Frank Morris.

The Legacy of the Alcatraz Escape

The Alcatraz escape has left a lasting legacy, not just as a fascinating historical event, but also as a symbol of human ingenuity, determination, and the desire for freedom. The escapees' meticulous planning and execution demonstrated that even the most secure prisons are not infallible. Their story continues to inspire both awe and curiosity, as people wonder whether the men succeeded in their quest for freedom or met a watery grave in the bay.

The escape also had significant repercussions for the U.S. prison system. Alcatraz, already under scrutiny for its harsh conditions and high operating costs, was closed just over a year after the escape, in 1963. The federal government recognized that the aging facility was no longer suitable for housing the nation's most dangerous criminals. The remaining inmates were transferred to other prisons, and Alcatraz was abandoned.

Today, Alcatraz Island is a popular tourist destination, drawing visitors from around the world who are eager to learn about its history and the infamous escape. The prison's dilapidated cells, crumbling walls, and haunting atmosphere provide a glimpse into the harsh realities of life on "The Rock." The story of the Alcatraz escape is a central part of the island's lore, with exhibits and tours dedicated to the men who dared to defy the odds.

The escape also continues to be a subject of ongoing research and investigation. Over the years, advances in forensic science and technology have led to new theories and discoveries related to the escape. Some investigators believe that the men may have had outside help, possibly from criminal contacts on the mainland. Others have analyzed the tides and currents in the bay, attempting to reconstruct the escape route and determine the likelihood of survival.

Despite the many questions that remain unanswered, the Alcatraz escape stands as a testament to the enduring human spirit and the relentless pursuit of freedom. Whether Frank Morris and the Anglin brothers survived or not, their daring escape has become an indelible part of American folklore. The mystery surrounding their fate ensures that the story of the Alcatraz escape will continue to be told for generations to come.

Chapter 4: Papillon

Henri Charrière, widely known by his nickname "Papillon," is a figure whose life story has become synonymous with the struggle for freedom against insurmountable odds. His autobiographical novel *Papillon*, published in 1969, recounts his harrowing experiences in the French penal colony of French Guiana and his daring escape attempts. The book became an international bestseller, later adapted into films that further immortalized his story. Papillon's tale is a gripping saga of resilience, survival, and the indomitable human spirit in the face of extreme adversity.

Early Life and Conviction

Henri Charrière was born on November 16, 1906, in Ardèche, France. Raised in a rural environment, Charrière was known for his rebellious nature from a young age. After serving in the French Navy, he returned to civilian life and quickly became involved in the Parisian underworld. He earned the nickname "Papillon" (French for "butterfly") because of a butterfly tattoo on his chest. Papillon became a small-time criminal, engaging in petty thefts, scams, and other illicit activities.

In 1931, Charrière was arrested and convicted of the murder of a Parisian pimp named Roland Legrand, a crime he always vehemently denied committing. Despite his protests of innocence, Charrière was sentenced to life in prison and hard labor in the French penal colony in French Guiana, a notorious prison system known for its brutal conditions and the near impossibility of escape. The most infamous of these prisons was Devil's Island, a remote and isolated island used to house the most dangerous and hardened criminals.

The Penal Colony of French Guiana

The French penal colony in French Guiana was established in the mid-19th century and became one of the most feared prison systems in the world. The colony consisted of several prisons, including the infamous Devil's Island, Saint-Laurent-du-Maroni, and Îles du Salut. Conditions in these prisons were harsh and inhumane, with prisoners subjected to extreme physical labor, malnutrition, disease, and abuse by guards. The dense jungle, swamps, and shark-infested waters surrounding the islands made escape nearly impossible, and many prisoners perished within the first few years of their sentences.

Devil's Island, located about 10 miles off the coast of French Guiana, was the most feared of all the prison facilities. It was reserved for political prisoners and the most dangerous criminals. The island's isolation, combined with the harsh tropical climate and the brutal treatment of prisoners, made it a living hell for those who were sent there. The prison became a symbol of the cruelty and despair of the French penal system.

For Papillon, the prospect of spending the rest of his life in such a place was unbearable. From the moment he arrived in French Guiana in 1933, he was determined to escape, no matter the cost. His story, as recounted in his autobiography, is a testament to his unwavering resolve and his refusal to be broken by the system.

The First Escape Attempts

Papillon's first escape attempt came just months after his arrival at the Saint-Laurent-du-Maroni prison in French Guiana. He and a fellow prisoner, Clousiot, hatched a plan to escape by boat. They managed to acquire a small boat and, along with two other prisoners, set out to sea. However, their boat was poorly equipped, and the group soon found themselves struggling against the powerful currents and rough seas of the Atlantic Ocean. After several days adrift, they were forced to land on the coast of Venezuela, where they were captured by Venezuelan authorities and returned to French Guiana.

Undeterred by this setback, Papillon continued to plan and execute escape attempts. He used every opportunity to gather information, make contacts, and secure resources that could aid in his escape. Over the years, he became known for his resourcefulness, cunning, and relentless determination to regain his freedom.

Papillon's second major escape attempt occurred in 1934 when he and eight other prisoners managed to escape from the Saint-Joseph prison, another facility within the penal colony. The group fled into the dense jungle, hoping to make their way to the Brazilian border. However, the harsh conditions of the jungle, combined with the lack of supplies and the constant threat of capture, quickly took their toll. The group eventually split up, and Papillon was once again captured by local authorities and returned to prison.

Despite these failures, Papillon never gave up on his dream of escaping. He continued to make plans and bide his time, waiting for the right moment to strike.

The Solitary Confinement Years

As punishment for his repeated escape attempts, Papillon was sentenced to a lengthy period of solitary confinement on Île Saint-Joseph, one of the smaller islands in the Îles du Salut group. Solitary confinement was one of the most severe punishments in the French penal system, designed to break the spirit of prisoners through isolation, deprivation, and psychological torment.

For two years, Papillon endured the harsh conditions of solitary confinement. His cell was a small, windowless room, with barely enough space to move. He was given minimal food, and contact with other prisoners was strictly forbidden. The isolation and sensory deprivation were intended to crush the will of the prisoner, reducing them to a state of hopelessness and despair.

However, Papillon's spirit was not easily broken. He used the time in solitary confinement to strengthen his resolve, refusing to let the conditions defeat him. He maintained his physical fitness by exercising in the limited space of his cell and kept his mind sharp by planning future escape attempts. He also found solace in the occasional contact with other prisoners, communicating with them by tapping on the walls of his cell.

After two years in solitary confinement, Papillon was finally released back into the general prison population. Far from being broken, he emerged more determined than ever to escape from the island.

The Final Escape: The Leap from Devil's Island

Papillon's most famous and successful escape attempt occurred in 1941 when he was transferred to the infamous Devil's Island. The island, located off the coast of French Guiana, was surrounded by treacherous waters filled with strong currents and dangerous marine life. It was considered inescapable, and the prisoners who were sent there were often left to die.

Despite the overwhelming odds, Papillon was undeterred. He began to devise a plan to escape from the island, using his knowledge of the sea and his resourcefulness to his advantage. He noticed that the strong currents around the island flowed in a specific direction, creating a potential escape route for someone brave enough to take the risk.

Papillon constructed a makeshift raft using sacks filled with coconuts, which he believed would keep him buoyant in the water. On a moonless night in 1941, he made his daring escape. He leaped from the cliffs of Devil's Island into the sea, clutching his coconut raft. The strong currents carried him away from the island, and after several hours of battling the waves, he reached the mainland of French Guiana.

Exhausted but alive, Papillon made his way through the jungle to find freedom. He eventually reached the coast of Venezuela, where he was taken in by a local indigenous tribe. The tribe cared for him and helped him recover from the physical and mental toll of his escape. After spending several months with the tribe, Papillon made his way to Caracas, the capital of Venezuela, where he finally achieved his long-sought freedom.

Life After Prison

After his escape, Papillon settled in Venezuela, where he married a Venezuelan woman and started a new life. He found work in various jobs, including as a mechanic, and eventually opened a restaurant in Caracas. He lived a relatively quiet and peaceful life, far from the horrors of the French penal colony that had haunted him for so many years.

In the late 1960s, Papillon decided to write his autobiography, recounting his experiences in the French penal colony and his numerous escape attempts. The book, *Papillon*, was published in 1969 and became an instant bestseller. The gripping and harrowing tale of his life captivated readers around the world, and Papillon became a symbol of the human spirit's resilience and determination to overcome even the direst circumstances.

The success of the book led to further adaptations of Papillon's story. In 1973, a film adaptation of *Papillon* was released, starring Steve McQueen as Henri Charrière and Dustin Hoffman as his fellow inmate Louis Dega. The film was a critical and commercial success, further cementing Papillon's place in popular culture.

Controversies and Criticisms

While *Papillon* was widely celebrated as a remarkable story of survival and escape, it also faced criticism and controversy. Some critics questioned the accuracy of Papillon's account, suggesting that certain events in the book were exaggerated or fictionalized. There were also claims that Papillon had incorporated the experiences of other prisoners into his own story, blurring the line between fact and fiction.

Despite these criticisms, Papillon maintained that his story was true, though he acknowledged that some details may have been altered or embellished for narrative effect. He defended his book as a memoir rather than a strictly factual account, arguing that it captured the essence of his experiences and the spirit of his struggle for freedom.

In the years following the publication of *Papillon*, several historians and researchers investigated the events described in the book. While some elements of the story were found to be consistent with historical records, others were more difficult to verify. The debate over the accuracy of Papillon's account has continued to this day, with some viewing it as a largely factual memoir and others as a work of historical fiction.

Papillon's Legacy

Henri Charrière passed away on July 29, 1973, just a few years after the publication of *Papillon*. Despite the controversies surrounding his story, he left behind a legacy that has endured for decades. Papillon's tale of survival, resilience, and the quest for freedom continues to inspire readers and audiences around the world.

The story of Papillon is not just about one man's struggle to escape from a brutal prison system; it is a testament to the power of the human spirit to overcome even the most extreme adversity. Papillon's determination, resourcefulness, and refusal to give up in the face of overwhelming odds have made him a symbol of hope and courage for those who find themselves in seemingly impossible situations.

In the years since his death, Papillon's story has continued to resonate with people of all ages and backgrounds. It has been adapted into films, plays, and other forms of media, ensuring that the legend of Henri Charrière, the man who refused to be caged, lives on.

Whether seen as a true account or a partially fictionalized narrative, the story of Papillon remains one of the most compelling and enduring tales of escape and survival in modern history. It serves as a reminder that even in the darkest of times, the human spirit is capable of extraordinary feats of courage and determination.

Chapter 5: Escape from Sobibor

The Escape from Sobibor stands as one of the most remarkable and heroic acts of resistance during the Holocaust. Sobibor was one of the Nazi death camps located in German-occupied Poland, designed explicitly for the extermination of Jews as part of the "Final Solution." Unlike concentration camps, where prisoners were subjected to forced labor, Sobibor was a death factory where tens of thousands of Jews were murdered in gas chambers shortly after their arrival. However, on October 14, 1943, a group of courageous Jewish prisoners orchestrated one of the most significant and successful uprisings of the Holocaust, leading to the mass escape of around 300 prisoners. This act of defiance not only disrupted the Nazi killing machine but also served as a powerful symbol of resistance and the indomitable human spirit.

The Sobibor Death Camp: A History of Horror

Sobibor was one of three Operation Reinhard camps, alongside Belzec and Treblinka, constructed by Nazi Germany for the systematic extermination of Jews. Operation Reinhard, named after SS General Reinhard Heydrich, was the code name for the Nazi plan to murder the Jews of Poland. Sobibor was located in a remote area near the village of Sobibor in the Lublin District of Poland, chosen for its seclusion, making it easier for the Nazis to carry out their atrocities away from public scrutiny.

Sobibor began operations in May 1942, and over the next 18 months, it became the site of unspeakable horrors. Jews from across Europe, including Poland, the Netherlands, France, and the Soviet Union, were transported to Sobibor in cattle cars. Upon arrival, most prisoners were immediately led to the gas chambers, disguised as showers, where they were murdered with carbon monoxide poisoning. The camp's efficiency as a death factory was chilling, with an estimated 250,000 Jews killed at Sobibor during its operation.

A small number of prisoners were selected to work in the camp, performing various tasks such as sorting the belongings of those murdered, disposing of bodies, and maintaining the camp's infrastructure. These prisoners were kept alive only as long as they were useful to the Nazis. The constant threat of death hung over them, and their lives were characterized by unimaginable brutality, fear, and despair.

The Spark of Resistance

Despite the overwhelming despair and the brutal conditions of the camp, a spark of resistance began to grow among the prisoners. The will to survive and the desire to defy their captors became a powerful force, fueling the determination to escape. The realization that the only way to survive was to escape became increasingly apparent, especially as news spread that the Nazis intended to liquidate the camp and destroy all evidence of their crimes.

The seeds of the Sobibor uprising were sown in the minds of a few key individuals, including Leon Feldhendler, a Polish Jewish prisoner who had been a leader in the Lublin ghetto before being deported to Sobibor. Feldhendler, along with other prisoners, began to discuss the possibility of organizing a mass escape. However, the plan needed a leader with military experience to give it a fighting chance of success.

That leader arrived in September 1943 in the form of Alexander "Sasha" Pechersky, a Soviet Jewish prisoner of war who had been captured by the Germans and deported to Sobibor. Pechersky was a Red Army officer with combat experience, and his arrival was a turning point in the planning of the uprising. With Pechersky's leadership, the escape plan began to take shape, involving a detailed and coordinated effort to kill the SS guards and escape en masse.

The Plan and Preparation

The escape plan devised by Pechersky and Feldhendler was audacious and fraught with danger. The camp was heavily guarded by SS officers and Ukrainian auxiliaries, and the surrounding area was filled with minefields, barbed wire, and watchtowers. The prisoners knew that even if they managed to overpower the guards and breach the camp's defenses, their chances of survival in the forests and swamps surrounding Sobibor were slim. Yet, the alternative—certain death in the gas chambers—left them with no choice.

The plan called for the secret assassination of the SS officers in the camp, one by one, in a coordinated operation. The prisoners intended to lure the officers into workshops or other isolated areas where they would be killed with tools, knives, or other makeshift weapons. Once a sufficient number of SS officers had been eliminated, the prisoners would seize the guards' weapons, cut through the camp's fences, and escape into the surrounding forests.

The plan required meticulous preparation and absolute secrecy. The risk of betrayal was high, and any hint of the plan reaching the ears of the SS would lead to its immediate failure and the execution of all involved. The prisoners involved in the planning formed small, trusted groups, and communication was conducted through a network of informants who passed messages using subtle signals and code words.

The day of the escape was set for October 14, 1943. The prisoners knew that they were racing against time, as the Nazis had begun dismantling the camp, and the likelihood of being killed increased with each passing day. The success of the plan hinged on timing, coordination, and the element of surprise.

The Day of the Uprising

On the morning of October 14, 1943, the plan was set in motion. The prisoners went about their daily tasks, concealing their anxiety and fear, knowing that their lives depended on the success of the operation. Pechersky, Feldhendler, and the other leaders quietly coordinated the final details, ensuring that each prisoner involved knew their role.

The first phase of the plan began in the afternoon, as the prisoners lured several SS officers into workshops and other isolated areas under the pretext of performing routine tasks. In a series of swift and silent attacks, the prisoners killed the officers using knives, axes, and hammers. The bodies were quickly hidden to avoid raising suspicion among the remaining guards.

As the number of dead SS officers grew, the prisoners seized their weapons and began to arm themselves. However, the plan did not go entirely smoothly. Some SS officers were able to escape the initial attacks, raising the alarm and alerting the remaining guards. The element of surprise was lost, and the camp descended into chaos.

Realizing that the situation was rapidly deteriorating, Pechersky gave the order for the prisoners to make a break for the camp's perimeter. Hundreds of prisoners, many of whom were unarmed, began to rush toward the barbed wire fences that surrounded the camp. Under heavy gunfire from the guards, the prisoners used makeshift ladders, their hands, and sheer force of will to break through the fences.

Once outside the camp, the prisoners scattered in all directions, running for the cover of the surrounding forests. The escapees faced immediate challenges: the minefields surrounding the camp, the pursuit of SS officers and local collaborators, and the harsh wilderness of the region. Many were killed by mines, shot by pursuing guards, or captured by local collaborators and Nazi patrols. Despite these challenges, around 300 prisoners managed to escape the camp, a remarkable feat considering the formidable odds they faced.

The Aftermath and Legacy of the Escape

Of the 300 prisoners who escaped Sobibor, only about 50 to 70 survived the war. Many of those who initially escaped were recaptured and executed, while others perished from the harsh conditions in the forests or at the hands of hostile locals. However, those who did survive lived to tell the tale of the Sobibor uprising, ensuring that the world would know of the courage and determination of the prisoners who dared to defy their Nazi captors.

The Sobibor uprising had a significant impact on the Nazi regime's operations. The successful escape and the subsequent discovery of the camp's dismantling by the escaping prisoners prompted Heinrich Himmler, one of the principal architects of the Holocaust, to order the immediate closure of Sobibor. The Nazis attempted to erase all evidence of the camp's existence, demolishing the gas chambers and other structures and planting trees over the site. Despite these efforts, the memory of Sobibor and the heroism of its prisoners could not be erased.

The story of the Sobibor escape has been preserved through the testimonies of survivors, historical research, and cultural representations. Among the most notable accounts is the book *Escape from Sobibor* by Richard Rashke, which provides a detailed chronicle of the uprising based on interviews with survivors. The book was later adapted into a television film in 1987, further cementing the legacy of the Sobibor escape in the collective memory of the Holocaust.

The Sobibor escape is a powerful reminder of the resilience and bravery of those who resisted the Nazi regime, even in the face of almost certain death. It is a testament to the strength of the human spirit and the unyielding desire for freedom, even in the darkest of times. The prisoners who participated in the Sobibor uprising knew that their chances of survival were slim, yet they chose to fight back, to reclaim their dignity, and to defy their oppressors. Their actions continue to inspire and resonate with people around the world, serving as a symbol of hope and resistance against tyranny and oppression.

The Commemoration of Sobibor

In the decades since the end of World War II, efforts have been made to commemorate the victims and survivors of Sobibor. The site of the former camp is now a memorial, with monuments, plaques, and exhibits dedicated to preserving the memory of those who perished there. The Sobibor memorial includes a museum that educates visitors about the history of the camp, the horrors of the Holocaust, and the courageous actions of the prisoners who fought for their freedom.

In recent years, archaeological excavations at the Sobibor site have uncovered additional evidence of the camp's operations, including remnants of the gas chambers, personal belongings of the victims, and mass graves. These findings have provided further insight into the scale of the atrocities committed at Sobibor and have reinforced the importance of preserving the site as a place of remembrance and education.

The Sobibor escape is not just a historical event; it is a story that continues to resonate with contemporary audiences. It serves as a reminder of the importance of resistance in the face of injustice, the value of human dignity, and the enduring power of hope. The legacy of the Sobibor escape lives on in the memories of the survivors, the education of future generations, and the ongoing efforts to honor those who fought for their freedom.

As we remember the Sobibor escape, we are reminded of the countless other acts of resistance that took place during the Holocaust, many of which have been forgotten or overlooked. The story of Sobibor is a testament to the fact that even in the darkest times, there are those who will stand up and fight for what is right, who will refuse to be broken by oppression, and who will seek freedom at any cost.

In conclusion, the Escape from Sobibor is a powerful and enduring symbol of resistance against the horrors of the Holocaust. It is a story of extraordinary courage, determination, and the unbreakable will to survive. The prisoners who escaped from Sobibor on October 14, 1943, not only reclaimed their freedom but also struck a blow against the Nazi regime, demonstrating that even in the face of overwhelming odds, the human spirit cannot be extinguished. Their legacy continues to inspire and challenge us to remember the past and to strive for a world where such atrocities are never repeated.

Chapter 6: Colditz Castle

Colditz Castle, a formidable fortress located in the town of Colditz in Saxony, Germany, is one of the most famous prisoner-of-war (POW) camps of World War II. Its name has become synonymous with daring escapes, cunning ingenuity, and the unbreakable spirit of Allied officers held captive within its walls. The castle's history is steeped in tales of bravery, creativity, and the relentless pursuit of freedom by the men imprisoned there.

Colditz Castle's story is not just one of confinement but of resilience, defiance, and the human drive to overcome even the most insurmountable odds. During the war, the castle became a focal point of intrigue and drama, where some of the most audacious escape attempts were conceived and executed. These attempts, many of which were successful, have since entered the annals of wartime legend, earning Colditz a unique place in military history.

The Origins of Colditz Castle

The history of Colditz Castle dates back to the Middle Ages. The castle, perched on a rocky promontory above the River Mulde, was originally built as a medieval fortress in the 11th century. Over the centuries, it underwent numerous expansions and renovations, transforming from a defensive stronghold into a Renaissance palace and later into a royal hunting lodge.

By the 19th century, Colditz Castle had fallen into disrepair and was repurposed as a psychiatric asylum. Its robust walls and remote location made it an ideal site for housing individuals considered dangerous or difficult to manage. The castle's imposing structure and strategic position would later make it an attractive choice for the German military as a high-security POW camp during World War II.

Colditz as a POW Camp

During World War II, Colditz Castle was designated Oflag IV-C, a high-security POW camp for captured Allied officers who had made repeated escape attempts from other camps or who were considered "incorrigible" by the Germans. The Nazis believed that the castle's isolated location, surrounded by steep cliffs and dense forests, combined with its thick stone walls and watchtowers, made it virtually escape-proof.

The first prisoners arrived at Colditz in November 1939, shortly after the outbreak of the war. Initially, the camp housed Polish officers, but as the war progressed, it became home to officers from various Allied nations, including Britain, France, Belgium, the Netherlands, and later the United States. Many of these officers were highly resourceful and determined to escape, making Colditz a hotbed of escape activity.

The Germans were acutely aware of the reputation Colditz was developing as an "escape-proof" fortress and took every precaution to ensure that it remained so. The camp was heavily guarded, with sentries patrolling the perimeter, searchlights illuminating the grounds at night, and regular roll calls to account for the prisoners. The guards, known as the Wehrmacht, were vigilant and often suspicious, aware that they were dealing with some of the most determined escape artists of the war.

The Spirit of Resistance: Life Inside Colditz

Life inside Colditz was harsh and monotonous, with strict routines, limited rations, and little contact with the outside world. However, the prisoners quickly adapted to their new environment, forming a tight-knit community that revolved around one central goal: escape. The officers imprisoned at Colditz were not ordinary soldiers; many were elite military personnel with a strong sense of duty, honor, and a burning desire to return to the fight against the Nazis.

The prisoners used their time in captivity to plot elaborate escape attempts, using whatever materials they could find to fashion tools, disguises, and even fake documents. The creativity and ingenuity displayed by the prisoners were extraordinary, as they devised numerous ways to outwit their captors and evade detection. This spirit of resistance was a constant source of tension between the prisoners and the guards, as the Germans sought to maintain control while the prisoners continually sought ways to undermine it.

Despite the harsh conditions, life in Colditz was not entirely devoid of activities. The prisoners organized educational classes, lectures, and even theatrical performances to keep their minds sharp and their spirits high. They created a microcosm of society within the castle walls, complete with its own hierarchy, committees, and regulations. This sense of order and purpose was crucial in maintaining morale and unity among the prisoners, fostering an environment where collaboration and mutual support were key to survival and the pursuit of escape.

Ingenious Escape Attempts: Creativity Behind Bars

The legend of Colditz is primarily built on the numerous daring and ingenious escape attempts that took place within its walls. Despite the castle's reputation as being escape-proof, the prisoners at Colditz were relentless in their efforts to break free. These attempts were characterized by their creativity, meticulous planning, and, often, their sheer audacity.

One of the most famous escapes from Colditz involved the construction of a glider, known as the "Colditz Cock." The idea for the glider was conceived by two British officers, Tony Rolt and Bill Goldfinch, who were both engineers. Using materials scavenged from the castle, including bed sheets, floorboards, and even porridge as glue, the prisoners secretly constructed the glider in the attic of the castle. The plan was to launch the glider from the roof of the castle and glide across the River Mulde to freedom. Although the glider was never used due to the liberation of the camp by American forces in April 1945, its construction remains one of the most remarkable feats of ingenuity during the war.

Another notable escape attempt involved a group of French officers who dug a tunnel from the castle's chapel. The tunnel, which took nine months to complete, was painstakingly excavated using spoons, knives, and other improvised tools. The prisoners disposed of the excavated earth by hiding it in the rafters of the chapel and in false compartments in their clothing. On the night of their escape, the officers successfully tunneled out of the castle and made their way to freedom. Unfortunately, they were recaptured just a few days later, but their efforts demonstrated the determination and resourcefulness of the Colditz prisoners.

Disguises also played a crucial role in many escape attempts. The prisoners at Colditz became masters of disguise, using stolen uniforms, civilian clothing, and even makeup to alter their appearances. One British officer, Airey Neave, successfully escaped by dressing as a German officer. Neave spoke fluent German and was able to pass through multiple checkpoints before making his way to neutral Switzerland. Neave later became the first British officer to successfully escape from Colditz and reach England.

In addition to individual efforts, there were also several mass escape attempts, where multiple prisoners coordinated their actions to overwhelm the guards or create distractions. One such attempt involved a group of prisoners who planned to hijack a German supply truck and drive it through the castle gates. The plan nearly succeeded, but the truck became stuck in the gatehouse, leading to the recapture of the prisoners involved. Despite the failure, this attempt highlighted the boldness and audacity of the Colditz prisoners, who were willing to take significant risks in their pursuit of freedom.

The Role of Espionage and Intelligence

The prisoners at Colditz were not only focused on escape; they were also engaged in a covert war of intelligence gathering and espionage. Many of the officers held at Colditz were privy to sensitive information and used their time in captivity to gather intelligence on the German war effort. The prisoners established secret communications networks, using hidden radios and coded messages to transmit information to the Allied forces.

One of the most remarkable intelligence operations involved the use of a secret radio transmitter, which the prisoners constructed from parts scavenged from the castle. The radio, hidden in a false wall, allowed the prisoners to listen to BBC broadcasts and keep informed about the progress of the war. The information gathered from these broadcasts was shared among the prisoners and used to coordinate escape attempts and other acts of resistance.

In addition to gathering intelligence, the prisoners at Colditz also engaged in acts of sabotage. They would intentionally damage equipment, disrupt communication lines, and create confusion among the German guards. These acts of defiance, though small in scale, contributed to the overall effort to undermine the German war machine and maintain the morale of the Allied prisoners.

Liberation and the End of the War

As the war drew to a close, the situation at Colditz became increasingly tense. The German guards, aware that the Allied forces were advancing, became more paranoid and desperate. The prisoners, sensing that liberation was near, intensified their escape efforts, knowing that any day could be their last opportunity to break free.

On April 16, 1945, American forces liberated Colditz Castle, bringing an end to the prisoners' captivity. The liberation was a moment of triumph for the Allied officers who had endured years of confinement, deprivation, and constant danger. For many, the experience of Colditz would leave a lasting impact, shaping their post-war lives and careers.

The Legacy of Colditz Castle

The story of Colditz Castle and the remarkable escape attempts that took place within its walls have left an indelible mark on history. The castle has become a symbol of resistance, ingenuity, and the unyielding human spirit in the face of adversity. The men who were imprisoned there demonstrated extraordinary courage, creativity, and determination, refusing to be broken by their captors.

In the years following the war, Colditz Castle became a subject of fascination and intrigue, inspiring numerous books, films, and television series. The memoirs of former prisoners, such as Airey Neave's *Colditz: A Story of Escape* and Pat Reid's *The Colditz Story*, have provided first-hand accounts of life inside the fortress and the daring escapes that took place. These accounts have helped to cement Colditz's reputation as one of the most infamous and legendary POW camps of World War II.

Today, Colditz Castle is a museum and memorial, dedicated to preserving the history of the POW camp and honoring the memory of those who were imprisoned there. Visitors can explore the castle's various rooms, including the attic where the Colditz Cock was constructed, the chapel where the French tunnel was dug, and the escape museum, which houses artifacts and exhibits related to the escapes.

The legacy of Colditz Castle serves as a reminder of the resilience of the human spirit and the lengths to which people will go to secure their freedom. The story of Colditz is not just a tale of captivity and escape; it is a testament to the power of hope, the importance of solidarity, and the enduring quest for liberty.

Chapter 7: The Great Escape

"The Great Escape" is one of the most legendary and audacious prison breaks in history, an event that has captured the imagination of people around the world and has been immortalized in books, documentaries, and a classic Hollywood film. This extraordinary escape took place during World War II at Stalag Luft III, a German prisoner-of-war camp designed to hold captured Allied airmen. The escape, executed by a group of determined prisoners, was a meticulously planned and executed operation that involved digging three long tunnels beneath the camp and culminated in a mass breakout of seventy-six men on the night of March 24-25, 1944. Despite its partial success and the tragic aftermath, the Great Escape remains a powerful symbol of courage, ingenuity, and the relentless human desire for freedom.

Stalag Luft III: The Setting for a Historic Escape

Stalag Luft III was a Luftwaffe-run POW camp located near the town of Sagan (now Żagań, Poland), approximately 100 miles southeast of Berlin. The camp was specifically built to house Allied airmen who had been captured during the war, including pilots, navigators, and aircrew members from various countries, primarily Britain, Canada, and the United States. Stalag Luft III was considered one of the most secure POW camps in Nazi Germany, with special design features aimed at preventing escape.

The camp was situated on sandy soil, which made tunneling difficult, and the barracks were raised off the ground to make it easier for guards to spot any digging activity. The perimeter of the camp was surrounded by high barbed wire fences, guard towers, and searchlights, making any escape attempt seem almost impossible. However, the prisoners at Stalag Luft III were highly resourceful and determined to defy the odds.

By the time of the Great Escape, the camp housed thousands of POWs, many of whom were experienced in escape techniques. These men had a strong sense of duty to continue the fight against the Nazis, even while in captivity, and viewed escape as their primary mission. The German guards, known as the "Goons," were well aware of the prisoners' reputation for escaping, and security was tight. Despite this, the prisoners formed an escape committee, known as "X Organization" or simply "X," led by Squadron Leader Roger Bushell, a charismatic and determined British officer who became the mastermind behind the Great Escape.

The Mastermind: Roger Bushell and "X Organization"

Roger Bushell, codenamed "Big X," was the driving force behind the Great Escape. Born in South Africa and educated in Britain, Bushell was a fighter pilot in the Royal Air Force (RAF) who had been shot down and captured in 1940. His intense desire to escape from German captivity and return to the fight was matched by his leadership skills and ability to inspire others. Bushell had already made several escape attempts from other camps before being sent to Stalag Luft III, where he quickly became the leader of the escape committee.

Under Bushell's leadership, X Organization set about planning one of the most ambitious escape attempts ever conceived. The plan called for the construction of three tunnels, codenamed "Tom," "Dick," and "Harry," which would be dug simultaneously to increase the chances of success. The idea was that if one tunnel was discovered, the other two could still be used. The goal was to break out a large number of prisoners—up to 200 men—who would then disperse across Europe, creating confusion for the German authorities and tying up resources in the search for them.

Bushell's plan was incredibly detailed and required the cooperation of hundreds of prisoners. Each man was assigned a specific role, from tunnel diggers to forgers who created fake documents, tailors who made civilian clothes, and "penguins" who discreetly disposed of the excavated soil by carrying it in small bags hidden in their trousers. The sheer scale of the operation was staggering, and it became known as the "Great Escape" even before it was executed.

The Tunnels: Tom, Dick, and Harry

The construction of the tunnels was a monumental task that required immense effort, secrecy, and ingenuity. The prisoners faced numerous challenges, including the sandy soil, which was prone to collapsing, and the constant threat of discovery by the guards. The tunnels were dug 30 feet below the surface to avoid detection by the guards and their listening devices. The tunnels were about 2 feet square, just large enough for a man to crawl through, and were reinforced with wood scavenged from beds, shelves, and even the walls of the barracks.

To ventilate the tunnels, the prisoners built an ingenious air pump system made from knapsacks and tin cans, which allowed fresh air to be circulated through the tunnels. Electric lights were also installed, powered by the camp's electricity supply, which the prisoners tapped into. The tunnels extended over 300 feet from the barracks to the woods beyond the camp's perimeter, a distance that required weeks of painstaking work to complete.

As the tunnels progressed, the prisoners used a variety of methods to conceal their activities. They built false walls and trapdoors to hide the entrances to the tunnels, and the excavated soil was carefully spread around the camp to avoid arousing suspicion. The "penguins" played a crucial role in this, as they would discreetly release small amounts of soil from hidden bags in their trousers while walking around the camp. This method, known as "penguining," was highly effective, but it also required careful coordination to avoid detection.

Despite the extensive precautions, the tunnel "Tom" was discovered by the guards in September 1943, forcing the prisoners to abandon it. However, work on "Harry" continued, and by March 1944, it was ready for use. "Dick," the third tunnel, was never used for an escape but served as a storage area for tools and materials.

The Night of the Escape: March 24-25, 1944

The night of the Great Escape was one of high tension and meticulous execution. On March 24, 1944, after months of preparation, the escape was set into motion. The prisoners knew that this was their best chance to break free, and every detail had been planned to maximize their chances of success.

The escape was scheduled to begin at night to avoid detection by the guards, with the first prisoners entering the tunnel around 10 p.m. The process was slow and arduous, as the men had to crawl through the narrow, claustrophobic tunnel in complete silence. The exit of the tunnel, which had been intended to emerge in the woods beyond the camp's perimeter, was discovered to be several feet short, leaving the prisoners dangerously exposed in an open area near the camp's fence.

Despite this setback, the prisoners pressed on, using ropes and signals to coordinate their movements. One by one, the men emerged from the tunnel and made their way into the surrounding woods, where they would change into civilian clothes and disperse into the German countryside. The plan was for the escapees to travel in small groups to increase their chances of evading capture. Some had forged documents, maps, and compasses, while others relied on their knowledge of the terrain and their ability to speak German or other European languages.

Unfortunately, the escape did not go as smoothly as planned. Delays in the tunnel, caused by a cave-in and a malfunctioning air pump, slowed the progress, and by the early hours of the morning, only seventy-six men had made it out. As the seventy-seventh man prepared to exit the tunnel, a German sentry noticed movement and raised the alarm, bringing the escape to an abrupt end. The camp was immediately put on lockdown, and a massive search was launched to recapture the fugitives.

The Aftermath: A Tragic Consequence

The aftermath of the Great Escape was both tragic and devastating. Of the seventy-six men who escaped, seventy-three were eventually recaptured by the Germans. Hitler, enraged by the escape, ordered that fifty of the captured men be executed as a deterrent to future escape attempts. This order, known as the "Sagan Order," was carried out with brutal efficiency. The fifty men, who included British, Canadian, and other Allied officers, were shot by the Gestapo and their bodies were cremated.

The execution of the fifty escapees was a war crime that shocked the world and brought international condemnation. The surviving prisoners at Stalag Luft III were devastated by the loss of their comrades, but they continued to resist the Germans in other ways, including acts of sabotage and intelligence gathering. The Allied governments vowed to bring those responsible for the executions to justice, and after the war, several Gestapo officers were tried and convicted for their roles in the murders.

Of the three men who successfully escaped and evaded capture, two were Norwegian pilots, Per Bergsland and Jens Müller, who made their way to neutral Sweden, and one was Dutch pilot Bram van der Stok, who reached the safety of Spain. These three men became heroes and symbols of the indomitable spirit of the Allied POWs.

The Legacy of the Great Escape

The Great Escape has left an enduring legacy that continues to inspire generations. The story of the escape, with its blend of heroism, ingenuity, and tragedy, has become a powerful symbol of resistance against tyranny and the unbreakable human will to achieve freedom. The escapees' determination to defy their captors, even at the risk of their lives, serves as a reminder of the sacrifices made by so many during the war.

The story was first brought to the public's attention through the 1950 book "The Great Escape" by Paul Brickhill, an Australian fighter pilot who was also a prisoner at Stalag Luft III and had been involved in the escape planning. Brickhill's book detailed the planning, execution, and aftermath of the escape and highlighted the bravery and ingenuity of the men involved.

In 1963, the story was further popularized by the Hollywood film "The Great Escape," directed by John Sturges and starring Steve McQueen, James Garner, and Richard Attenborough. Although the film took some liberties with the facts, it captured the essence of the escape and brought the story to a global audience. The film's iconic scenes, such as McQueen's character attempting to jump a barbed-wire fence on a motorcycle, have become legendary in their own right.

In the years since the escape, Stalag Luft III has been preserved as a historical site, with a museum dedicated to the Great Escape and the men who were held there. Visitors can see the remnants of the camp, including the location of the tunnels and the memorials to the fifty executed escapees. The story of the Great Escape is also commemorated in various books, documentaries, and exhibitions that continue to honor the bravery and sacrifice of those involved.

The Great Escape remains one of the most compelling and inspiring stories of World War II, a testament to the resilience of the human spirit and the enduring quest for freedom. It is a story that resonates across time and continues to remind us of the power of courage, determination, and hope in the face of overwhelming odds.

49

Chapter 8: Ted Bundy

Ted Bundy is one of the most infamous serial killers in American history, a figure whose name has become synonymous with deceit, charm, and unthinkable violence. His life and crimes have been the subject of countless books, documentaries, movies, and scholarly articles, each trying to unravel the complex personality behind his horrific actions. Bundy's criminal career spanned the 1970s, a decade in which he brutally murdered at least 30 young women across several states in the United States. The true number of his victims is unknown and may be much higher.

What makes Bundy a particularly chilling figure is not just the sheer number of his crimes but the manner in which he carried them out. Bundy was a master manipulator who used his charm, good looks, and intelligence to lure his victims to their deaths. His ability to mask his monstrous tendencies behind a facade of normalcy allowed him to evade capture for years, making him one of the most dangerous and elusive criminals of his time. This detailed account delves into the life, crimes, capture, and enduring legacy of Ted Bundy, exploring how a seemingly ordinary man became one of history's most terrifying serial killers.

Early Life and Background

Ted Bundy was born Theodore Robert Cowell on November 24, 1946, in Burlington, Vermont. His mother, Eleanor Louise Cowell, was unmarried at the time, and the identity of his father remains unclear. To avoid the stigma of illegitimacy, Bundy was raised as the son of his grandparents, Samuel and Eleanor Cowell, while his mother posed as his sister. This arrangement created a confusing and unsettling family dynamic, which some psychologists later speculated may have contributed to his disturbed psyche.

Bundy's early years were marked by an outward appearance of normalcy. He was described as a bright and polite child, though there were signs of darker tendencies even in his youth. He had a fascination with knives and reportedly engaged in animal cruelty, both behaviors often associated with future violent offenders. Despite these warning signs, Bundy's early life did not foreshadow the horrors he would later commit.

As a teenager, Bundy struggled with feelings of social inadequacy and rejection. Although he was intelligent and had a keen interest in law and politics, he found it difficult to form close relationships. His sense of alienation was compounded by the discovery of his true parentage, which reportedly left him feeling betrayed by those closest to him. This revelation may have deepened his resentment towards women, which would later manifest in his crimes.

After high school, Bundy attended the University of Puget Sound and later transferred to the University of Washington, where he studied psychology. During this time, he began a relationship with a woman named Stephanie Brooks (a pseudonym), who fit the profile of many of his later victims—young, attractive, with long dark hair parted in the middle. When Stephanie ended their relationship, Bundy was devastated. This rejection is often cited as a pivotal moment in his life, contributing to his growing hatred towards women.

The Emergence of a Killer

Bundy's criminal activities began in earnest in the early 1970s, though his first confirmed murders did not occur until 1974. By this time, he had developed a method of luring his victims that relied on his ability to appear trustworthy and harmless. Bundy would often pretend to be injured, using a sling or crutches to elicit sympathy from young women. Once they were close enough, he would overpower them, sometimes using a crowbar or other blunt instrument, before abducting and murdering them.

Bundy's victims were typically young, white, college-aged women with long hair parted in the middle, a fact that has led some to speculate that he was attempting to recreate the image of his first girlfriend, Stephanie Brooks. His murders were marked by extreme violence, often involving sexual assault, strangulation, and mutilation. Bundy would later confess to returning to the bodies of his victims to perform acts of necrophilia, further underscoring the depravity of his crimes.

Bundy's killing spree spanned multiple states, including Washington, Oregon, Utah, Colorado, and Florida. His ability to evade capture for so long was due in part to his nomadic lifestyle, as he moved from state to state to avoid detection. Additionally, Bundy was meticulous in covering his tracks, often disposing of bodies in remote locations and taking precautions to minimize the evidence left behind.

One of Bundy's most audacious crimes occurred in January 1975, when he abducted and murdered Caryn Campbell, a 23-year-old nurse, from a hotel in Aspen, Colorado. This crime, along with others in Colorado, led to his eventual arrest in Utah in August 1975 for the kidnapping of Carol DaRonch, a woman who managed to escape Bundy's clutches. DaRonch's testimony would later play a crucial role in securing Bundy's conviction.

Arrests and Escapes

Bundy's first arrest came in August 1975, when he was pulled over by police in Salt Lake City for driving erratically. During the traffic stop, officers discovered burglary tools in his car, which included handcuffs, a crowbar, a ski mask, and a pair of pantyhose with eyeholes cut out. This discovery led to his arrest on suspicion of attempted burglary, but police soon connected him to the attempted kidnapping of Carol DaRonch, who positively identified Bundy in a lineup.

In February 1976, Bundy was convicted of DaRonch's kidnapping and sentenced to 15 years in prison. However, this was far from the end of his criminal activities. While in custody, Bundy became a suspect in several unsolved murders in Colorado, and in 1977, he was extradited to Colorado to face charges for the murder of Caryn Campbell. It was during his time in Colorado that Bundy would execute two daring escapes, further cementing his notoriety.

Bundy's first escape occurred on June 7, 1977, when he was being held at the Pitkin County Courthouse in Aspen for a preliminary hearing. Bundy was permitted to use the law library to research his case and, taking advantage of the lax security, jumped out of a second-story window. He managed to evade capture for six days, hiding in the wilderness before being recaptured. Despite his escape attempt, Bundy remained determined to avoid facing justice, and on December 30, 1977, he executed his second, more successful escape.

This time, Bundy managed to saw through the ceiling of his cell in the Garfield County Jail in Glenwood Springs, Colorado, and climbed into the crawl space above. He then made his way to a closet in the jailer's apartment, changed into civilian clothes he had stolen, and walked out of the front door. Bundy's escape went unnoticed for over 15 hours, giving him a significant head start. He fled to Chicago and then to Tallahassee, Florida, where he would commit his final, most brutal murders.

The Florida Murders and Final Capture

Bundy arrived in Tallahassee in early January 1978, having successfully evaded law enforcement across multiple states. He assumed the alias "Chris Hagen" and rented a room at a boarding house near Florida

State University (FSU). However, Bundy's urge to kill was undiminished, and within days of his arrival, he launched a savage attack on the Chi Omega sorority house at FSU.

On the night of January 15, 1978, Bundy broke into the sorority house and brutally attacked four young women, killing two of them—Margaret Bowman and Lisa Levy. He bludgeoned his victims with a piece of firewood and strangled them, leaving behind a gruesome crime scene. Bundy then attacked two more women in a nearby apartment, Cheryl Thomas and Kathy Kleiner, both of whom survived but were severely injured.

The murders at the Chi Omega house shocked the nation and marked the beginning of the end for Bundy. Less than a month later, on February 9, 1978, Bundy abducted and murdered 12-year-old Kimberly Leach in Lake City, Florida. This crime, the abduction and murder of a child, would later be one of the charges that led to his death sentence.

Bundy's time on the run came to an end on February 15, 1978, when he was stopped by Pensacola police officer David Lee for driving a stolen vehicle. After a brief struggle, Bundy was arrested and taken into custody. This time, Bundy's luck had run out, and he would soon face the full force of the law.

The Trials and Sentencing

Ted Bundy's trials were among the most publicized in American history, drawing intense media attention and public fascination. The trial for the Chi Omega murders began in June 1979 in Miami, Florida, and was the first nationally televised trial in the United States. Bundy, who had a law degree from the University of Utah, chose to represent himself, further feeding the media circus surrounding the case.

During the trial, Bundy displayed the same charm and charisma that had allowed him to evade capture for so long, but the evidence against him was overwhelming. Prosecutors presented eyewitness testimony, physical evidence linking Bundy to the crime scenes, and bite mark analysis that matched Bundy's teeth to the wounds on Lisa Levy's body. Despite Bundy's attempts to manipulate the proceedings, the jury took less than seven hours to convict him of the murders of Margaret Bowman and Lisa Levy, as well as the attempted murders of Karen Chandler and Kathy Kleiner.

Bundy was sentenced to death by electrocution for the Chi Omega murders, a sentence that was affirmed by the Florida Supreme Court in 1980. However, his legal battles were far from over. In January 1980, Bundy was tried for the murder of Kimberly Leach, the 12-year-old girl he had abducted and killed. Once again, Bundy was convicted and sentenced to death.

Despite his death sentences, Bundy continued to manipulate the legal system, filing numerous appeals and delaying his execution for nearly a decade. During this time, he also confessed to many of his crimes, providing law enforcement with details about his murders in an attempt to avoid execution. Bundy's confessions were chilling, as he described the brutal and calculated nature of his killings, often with a disturbing lack of remorse.

Execution and Legacy

Ted Bundy was executed in the electric chair at Florida State Prison on January 24, 1989. His execution was witnessed by a large crowd of onlookers who gathered outside the prison, many of whom celebrated the death of the man who had terrorized the nation for so long. Bundy's execution marked the end of one of the most infamous criminal careers in American history, but his legacy of horror continues to haunt the public consciousness.

Bundy's crimes have left a lasting impact on the study of criminal behavior, particularly in the field of psychology. His ability to mask his true nature behind a facade of charm and intelligence has made him a subject of intense study, as experts seek to understand how someone who appeared so normal could commit such heinous acts. Bundy's case has also highlighted the importance of forensic science, as advances in technology have made it possible to solve cases that might have otherwise gone cold.

In popular culture, Bundy remains a figure of fascination and fear. His life and crimes have been the subject of numerous books, documentaries, and films, each attempting to explore the depths of his depravity and the psychology behind his actions. Notable portrayals include the 2002 film "Ted Bundy," the 2019 Netflix film "Extremely Wicked, Shockingly Evil and Vile," starring Zac Efron, and the documentary series "Conversations with a Killer: The Ted Bundy Tapes," which features interviews with Bundy himself.

While Bundy's name is now synonymous with evil, his story also serves as a cautionary tale about the dangers of underestimating those who present themselves as charming and trustworthy. His ability to exploit the trust of others, combined with his intelligence and meticulous planning, allowed him to carry out his crimes for years before he was finally brought to justice. The Ted Bundy case remains one of the most chilling examples of how the face of a killer can hide behind the mask of a seemingly ordinary man.

Chapter 9: Gary Tison

Gary Tison's name may not be as widely recognized as some of the more infamous criminals in American history, but his life and crimes are no less compelling or terrifying. Tison was a cold-blooded murderer, a master manipulator, and the orchestrator of one of the most notorious prison escapes in the United States. His story is one of violence, desperation, and the tragic consequences of a life lived outside the law. Over the course of his criminal career, Tison's actions led to the deaths of numerous individuals, including innocent bystanders, as he pursued a relentless quest for freedom at any cost.

This comprehensive account delves into the life of Gary Tison, exploring his troubled beginnings, his descent into criminality, his notorious prison escape, and the bloody aftermath that ensued. Tison's story is not just one of personal downfall but also a cautionary tale about the devastating impact of crime on both individuals and society.

Early Life and Criminal Beginnings

Gary Gene Tison was born on March 29, 1935, in Casa Grande, Arizona. Raised in a small rural community, Tison's early life was marked by hardship and instability. He came from a poor family and had a difficult upbringing, which some might argue contributed to his later criminal behavior. From a young age, Tison displayed a rebellious streak and a propensity for trouble. He had little interest in school and often found himself on the wrong side of the law.

Tison's first brushes with the law were relatively minor, involving petty theft and juvenile delinquency. However, as he grew older, his crimes escalated in both frequency and severity. By his late teens, Tison had graduated from petty crimes to more serious offenses, including burglary and armed robbery. His growing criminal record and increasingly violent tendencies made him a prime target for law enforcement.

In the early 1960s, Tison's criminal activities took a more sinister turn when he was involved in a botched robbery that ended in murder. In 1961, Tison and an accomplice, Randy Greenawalt, attempted to rob a store in Arizona. During the robbery, Tison shot and killed a man, marking his first known murder. This act of violence set the tone for the rest of Tison's life, as he would continue to use lethal force to achieve his goals.

Tison was quickly apprehended after the murder and sentenced to life in prison without the possibility of parole. However, his time behind bars would only serve to harden him further, as he began to plot his escape from the confines of the Arizona State Prison.

Life in Prison and the Quest for Freedom

Gary Tison's life sentence did little to quell his desire for freedom. While incarcerated, he quickly gained a reputation as a dangerous and manipulative inmate. He was known for his ability to charm and influence others, often using his persuasive skills to enlist the help of fellow inmates and even prison staff in his various schemes.

Tison's ability to manipulate those around him was particularly evident in his relationship with his wife, Dorothy. Despite his incarceration, Tison maintained a strong influence over Dorothy, who remained devoted to him throughout his time in prison. This devotion would later play a crucial role in Tison's escape plans, as Dorothy became an unwitting accomplice in her husband's quest for freedom.

Over the years, Tison attempted several escapes from prison, all of which were thwarted by prison authorities. However, these failed attempts only served to strengthen his resolve. Tison was determined to regain his freedom, no matter the cost, and he was willing to go to any lengths to achieve his goal.

In the late 1970s, Tison began to hatch a new escape plan, one that would involve not just his own freedom but that of his sons as well. By this time, Tison's sons, Donald, Ricky, and Raymond, had grown up and were deeply loyal to their father. Despite their father's criminal background, the Tison boys idolized him and were eager to help him escape from prison. This familial bond would prove to be a deadly combination, as the Tison family embarked on a crime spree that would shock the nation.

The 1978 Prison Escape

The events leading up to the 1978 prison escape began with Tison's meticulous planning and manipulation of those around him. Tison had managed to convince prison officials that he was a model inmate, even going so far as to establish a friendly relationship with the prison warden. This facade of good behavior earned him certain privileges, including access to areas of the prison that were typically off-limits to other inmates.

On July 30, 1978, Tison's sons, Donald, Ricky, and Raymond, visited him at the Arizona State Prison in Florence. During this visit, the Tison boys smuggled firearms into the prison, concealed within a large ice chest. The plan was simple but deadly: the Tison boys would hold the guards at gunpoint, allowing their father and his accomplice, Randy Greenawalt, to escape.

The plan went off without a hitch. The Tison boys overpowered the guards, securing their father's release. The group quickly fled the prison in a waiting vehicle, embarking on a violent and desperate journey that would leave a trail of bloodshed in its wake.

The Crime Spree and Murderous Rampage

After their successful escape, Gary Tison and his sons, along with Randy Greenawalt, embarked on a cross-country crime spree that would last for several weeks. The group initially headed north, robbing stores and stealing cars to fund their escape. However, their flight from justice soon turned deadly as they encountered a series of innocent victims who would lose their lives at the hands of the Tison gang.

The first victims of the Tison gang were a young married couple, John and Donnelda Lyons, and their two-year-old son, Christopher. The Lyons family was on a road trip when they encountered the Tison gang, who forced them off the road at gunpoint. The Tisons coldly executed the entire family, shooting them to death and leaving their bodies in the desert. The Tison gang then stole the family's car and continued their flight from justice.

The murder of the Lyons family marked the beginning of a bloody rampage that would claim the lives of several more innocent victims. Over the next few weeks, the Tison gang committed a series of robberies and murders as they traveled across the southwestern United States. Their crimes were marked by a complete disregard for human life, as they ruthlessly gunned down anyone who stood in their way.

As the Tison gang's crime spree continued, law enforcement agencies across multiple states launched a massive manhunt to capture the fugitives. The media quickly picked up on the story, and the Tison gang became one of the most wanted criminal groups in the country. Despite the intense pressure from law enforcement, the Tison gang managed to evade capture for several weeks, moving from one location to another in a desperate bid to stay ahead of the authorities.

The Final Showdown and Capture

The Tison gang's luck finally ran out on August 11, 1978, when they were cornered by law enforcement near Casa Grande, Arizona. A fierce gunfight ensued between the Tison gang and the police, during which Gary Tison's son, Donald, was fatally shot. The remaining members of the gang managed to escape into the desert, but the noose was tightening around them.

After days of searching, law enforcement finally tracked down the remaining members of the Tison gang on August 14, 1978. Ricky and Raymond Tison were captured without incident, but Gary Tison and Randy Greenawalt managed to flee into the remote Arizona desert. Despite the intense heat and harsh conditions, Tison and Greenawalt continued to evade capture for several more days.

Gary Tison's life of crime came to a tragic and ignominious end on August 20, 1978, when he was found dead in the desert, having succumbed to exposure and dehydration. His death marked the end of one of the most notorious crime sprees in American history, but the impact of his actions would be felt for years to come.

Randy Greenawalt was captured alive and later sentenced to death for his role in the murders committed during the escape. Greenawalt was executed by lethal injection in 1997. Ricky and Raymond Tison were also sentenced to death for their involvement in the crime spree, but their sentences were later commuted to life in prison without the possibility of parole.

Legacy and Impact

The story of Gary Tison and his family's crime spree is one of the most tragic and disturbing chapters in the history of American crime. Tison's ability to manipulate and control those around him, particularly his own sons, underscores the devastating impact that a life of crime can have on families and communities. The Tison gang's murderous rampage left a trail of destruction in its wake, claiming the lives of innocent victims and leaving a lasting scar on the collective memory of the nation.

In the years since the Tison gang's capture, their story has been the subject of numerous books, documentaries, and television specials. The case has been analyzed by criminologists and psychologists who seek to understand the motivations behind such extreme acts of violence. Tison's life and crimes continue to serve as a grim reminder of the dangers posed by those who are willing to go to any lengths to achieve their goals, regardless of the cost to others.

The legacy of Gary Tison is one of violence, desperation, and the tragic consequences of a life lived outside the law. His story serves as a cautionary tale about the dangers of unchecked criminal behavior and the devastating impact it can have on both individuals and society as a whole.

Chapter 10: John McCluskey

John McCluskey's name became synonymous with fear and brutality following his 2010 prison escape and the subsequent crime spree that gripped the United States. McCluskey, a hardened criminal with a violent past, orchestrated one of the most infamous escapes in recent history, leading to a nationwide manhunt that captivated the nation. His escape, coupled with the heinous crimes he committed while on the run, painted a chilling picture of a man who was willing to go to any lengths to avoid recapture. This comprehensive account delves deep into the life of John McCluskey, exploring his troubled beginnings, criminal evolution, the dramatic prison escape, and the violent aftermath that followed. The story of McCluskey is not just a tale of criminality but also a stark reminder of the dangers posed by individuals who live outside the boundaries of law and order.

Early Life and Descent into Criminality

John Charles McCluskey was born on February 12, 1965, in Arizona. From a young age, McCluskey's life was marked by turmoil and instability. Raised in a chaotic environment, he lacked the guidance and support that might have steered him away from a life of crime. As a child, McCluskey struggled with authority and often found himself in trouble at school and in his community. His rebellious nature and inability to conform to societal norms set the stage for a life defined by criminal behavior.

By his teenage years, McCluskey had already begun to amass a criminal record. His early offenses were relatively minor, involving theft and drug use. However, as he grew older, his crimes escalated in both frequency and severity. McCluskey's brushes with the law became more frequent, and his encounters with the criminal justice system became more severe. His inability to adhere to the rules of society ultimately led to his first stint in prison.

In the late 1980s, McCluskey was convicted of multiple felonies, including armed robbery, assault, and attempted murder. These convictions landed him in and out of prison throughout the 1990s and early 2000s. During his time behind bars, McCluskey became increasingly hardened, developing connections with other criminals and deepening his involvement in the criminal underworld. His time in prison only served to reinforce his belief that he was beyond redemption and that his life would forever be intertwined with crime.

The 2009 Conviction and Life Sentence

By 2009, McCluskey had been convicted of multiple violent crimes, including attempted second-degree murder, aggravated assault, and misconduct involving weapons. His criminal record was extensive, and he was considered a highly dangerous individual. As a result, he was sentenced to a lengthy prison term that effectively amounted to life behind bars. McCluskey was incarcerated at the Arizona State Prison Complex in Kingman, a medium-security facility that housed some of the state's most notorious criminals.

Despite the seemingly inescapable reality of spending the rest of his life in prison, McCluskey refused to accept his fate. He began to plot his escape, driven by a desperate desire to regain his freedom at any cost. The idea of spending the rest of his life in a cell was unbearable to him, and he was willing to go to extreme lengths to avoid that outcome.

The 2010 Prison Escape

On July 30, 2010, John McCluskey, along with fellow inmates Tracy Province and Daniel Renwick, orchestrated a daring escape from the Arizona State Prison Complex. The escape was made possible with the help of an accomplice on the outside, Casslyn Welch, who was

McCluskey's cousin and fiancée. Welch had been in a relationship with McCluskey and was deeply committed to helping him escape from prison.

Welch played a crucial role in the escape plan. She smuggled tools and weapons into the prison, which the inmates used to overpower a guard and cut through a fence. Once outside the prison, the trio made their way to a waiting vehicle, driven by Welch, and fled the scene. The escape was executed with precision and speed, leaving authorities scrambling to catch up.

The escape sparked a nationwide manhunt, as law enforcement agencies across the country worked to track down the fugitives. The escape was widely covered in the media, with McCluskey and his accomplices quickly becoming some of the most wanted criminals in the United States. Despite the intense search efforts, the fugitives managed to evade capture for several weeks, during which time they committed a series of violent crimes.

The Crime Spree and Murder of the Haas Family

Following their escape, McCluskey and his accomplices embarked on a crime spree that would leave a trail of destruction in its wake. The fugitives traveled across several states, robbing stores, stealing cars, and evading law enforcement at every turn. Their crime spree was marked by a complete disregard for human life, as they were willing to commit any act of violence necessary to avoid capture.

One of the most heinous crimes committed by McCluskey and his accomplices was the brutal murder of Gary and Linda Haas, an elderly couple from Tecumseh, Oklahoma. On August 2, 2010, the Haas family was traveling through New Mexico on a cross-country road trip when they encountered McCluskey and his group. The fugitives, desperate for a new vehicle, carjacked the Haas family at gunpoint.

McCluskey, Province, and Welch forced the couple into their camper and drove them to a remote location.

Once they reached a secluded area, McCluskey and his accomplices coldly executed Gary and Linda Haas, shooting them both in the head. After killing the couple, the fugitives set their camper on fire, burning the bodies in an attempt to destroy evidence. The murder of the Haas family was a senseless and brutal act that shocked the nation and underscored the dangerousness of the fugitives on the run.

The crime spree continued in the days following the Haas murders, as McCluskey and his group made their way across the country. Despite their efforts to stay ahead of the law, the fugitives were eventually cornered by authorities in Wyoming. Renwick, who had split from the group early on, was captured after a shootout with police in Colorado. Province, who had also separated from the group, was apprehended in Wyoming without incident. This left McCluskey and Welch as the last remaining fugitives.

The Capture and Aftermath

The nationwide manhunt for McCluskey and Welch came to an end on August 19, 2010, when the couple was apprehended at a campsite in northeastern Arizona. Acting on a tip from a concerned citizen, law enforcement surrounded the campsite and took McCluskey and Welch into custody without a fight. The capture of the fugitives brought relief to a nation that had been gripped by fear and uncertainty during the weeks-long manhunt.

Following his capture, McCluskey was extradited to New Mexico to stand trial for the murder of Gary and Linda Haas. In 2013, he was found guilty of capital murder and sentenced to life in prison without the possibility of parole. The trial was closely followed by the media, and McCluskey showed little remorse for his actions during the proceedings. His cold and callous demeanor in court only served to reinforce the public's perception of him as a dangerous and unrepentant criminal.

Casslyn Welch, who had played a key role in both the prison escape and the subsequent crime spree, was also convicted of multiple charges, including first-degree murder. She was sentenced to 40 years in prison for her involvement in the crimes. Tracy Province, who had been apprehended in Wyoming, was sentenced to life in prison without the possibility of parole. Daniel Renwick, who was captured after a shootout with police, was sentenced to 60 years in prison.

The Legacy of John McCluskey

The story of John McCluskey is one of desperation, violence, and the tragic consequences of a life lived outside the law. His 2010 prison escape and the subsequent crime spree left a lasting impact on the communities he terrorized and the families he destroyed. The senseless murders of Gary and Linda Haas serve as a grim reminder of the dangers posed by individuals like McCluskey, who are willing to commit any act of violence to achieve their goals.

McCluskey's escape and the crimes that followed also highlighted the vulnerabilities within the prison system and the need for greater security measures to prevent similar incidents in the future. The Arizona State Prison Complex, where McCluskey was incarcerated, faced significant scrutiny in the wake of the escape, with investigations revealing lapses in security and oversight that had allowed the escape to occur. The case led to calls for reforms within the prison system, including better training for staff and improved protocols for preventing escapes.

In the years since his capture, McCluskey has remained incarcerated, serving his life sentence without the possibility of parole. His name has become a symbol of the dark and violent path that some individuals take when they choose to live outside the bounds of law and order. The story of John McCluskey is a cautionary tale about the consequences of a life of crime and the devastating impact it can have on both individuals and society as a whole.

Chapter 11: Oklahoma Prison Escape

The Oklahoma Prison Escape is one of the most harrowing and violent prison escapes in recent American history. This daring escape involved a group of dangerous criminals who, fueled by desperation and a blatant disregard for human life, broke free from the confines of a high-security prison, leading to a manhunt that stretched across several states. The escape, which occurred in the early 21st century, not only highlighted the vulnerabilities within the prison system but also left a trail of terror in its wake as the fugitives committed a series of violent crimes during their brief taste of freedom. This comprehensive account delves into the origins of the escape, the backgrounds of the prisoners involved, the methodical planning and execution of the breakout, the ensuing crime spree, and the eventual recapture of the fugitives. The Oklahoma Prison Escape is a chilling reminder of the lengths to which some individuals will go to evade justice and the chaos that can ensue when the system fails to contain them.

Background: The Prison and Its Inmates

The Oklahoma State Penitentiary, located in McAlester, is one of the most notorious and secure prisons in the state. Known for housing some of the most dangerous criminals in Oklahoma, the facility is designed to keep its inmates under strict control, with high walls, razor wire fences, and heavily armed guards patrolling the perimeter. Despite these precautions, the prison has a long and troubled history, with several attempted escapes and incidents of violence occurring within its walls.

By the time of the escape in question, the penitentiary was home to a group of inmates who had little to lose. Among them were career criminals with long rap sheets, individuals who had spent most of their lives in and out of prison, and violent offenders who had been sentenced to long terms behind bars. These inmates, hardened by years of incarceration and embittered by the system, were united by a common goal: to regain their freedom at any cost.

Among the escapees were Charles Victor Thompson, a man with a history of violence, and Randolph Dial, a convicted murderer with a reputation for being a cunning and manipulative individual. Both men had been serving lengthy sentences for their crimes and had little hope of ever seeing the outside world again. This sense of desperation, coupled with their deep-seated resentment towards the prison system, set the stage for what would become one of the most audacious prison escapes in Oklahoma's history.

Planning the Escape: A Conspiracy of Desperation

The Oklahoma Prison Escape was not a spur-of-the-moment decision but rather the result of meticulous planning and preparation. The inmates involved spent months devising their plan, exploiting every weakness they could identify within the prison's security measures. Their plan hinged on a combination of cunning, deception, and brute force, and it would require the cooperation of several inmates who shared their desire for freedom.

One of the key elements of the escape plan involved securing outside help. The escapees knew that they would need assistance from someone who could provide them with the tools and resources necessary to break free. This is where the cunning and manipulative nature of Randolph Dial came into play. Dial, who was known for his ability to manipulate others, managed to gain the trust of Bobbi Parker, the wife of a prison warden. Through a combination of charm and coercion, Dial convinced Parker to assist in the escape, promising her a life of freedom and adventure away from the drudgery of prison life.

Parker's involvement in the escape was crucial. She provided the inmates with the tools they needed to cut through the prison's fences, including wire cutters and other implements. She also helped to smuggle contraband into the prison, including a handgun, which would later be used to intimidate guards during the escape. Parker's role in the escape would later become the subject of intense scrutiny and legal proceedings, with many questioning whether she had been a willing participant or a victim of Dial's manipulation.

The Escape: Breaking Free from the Prison Walls

The escape took place in the early hours of a cold winter morning, when the prison was at its quietest. The inmates, led by Thompson and Dial, put their plan into action with military precision. Armed with the tools and weapons provided by Parker, they began to cut through the fences that surrounded the prison. The process was slow and laborious, but the inmates worked with grim determination, knowing that this was their one chance at freedom.

As they made their way through the fences, the escapees encountered several obstacles, including locked gates and patrolling guards. However, they had anticipated these challenges and were prepared to deal with them. Using the handgun provided by Parker, the inmates overpowered a guard who happened upon them during the escape. The guard, fearing for his life, was forced to hand over his keys, which the inmates used to unlock the gates that stood between them and freedom.

Once outside the prison walls, the escapees made their way to a waiting vehicle that had been parked just outside the prison's perimeter. The vehicle, which had been stolen earlier in the night, was loaded with supplies that the inmates would need to survive on the run, including food, water, and additional weapons. The escapees quickly piled into the vehicle and sped away from the prison, leaving chaos and confusion in their wake.

The Manhunt: A Nationwide Search for the Fugitives

The escape from the Oklahoma State Penitentiary set off a nationwide manhunt, as law enforcement agencies across the country mobilized to track down the fugitives. The escapees were considered highly dangerous, and authorities feared that they would commit further acts of violence in their bid to evade capture. The manhunt involved hundreds of officers from various agencies, including the FBI, state police, and local law enforcement, all working together to bring the fugitives to justice.

The search for the escapees was complicated by the fact that they had a head start on the authorities. By the time the prison realized that the inmates were missing, the escapees had already driven several hundred miles away from the prison. They had also taken steps to cover their tracks, switching vehicles multiple times and avoiding major highways to evade detection.

The manhunt quickly became a high-profile case, with media outlets across the country providing extensive coverage of the search. The public was urged to remain vigilant and report any sightings of the fugitives, and a reward was offered for information leading to their capture. Despite these efforts, the escapees remained at large for several weeks, during which time they continued to commit crimes as they made their way across the country.

The Crime Spree: Violence and Desperation on the Run

As they fled from the law, the escapees embarked on a crime spree that left a trail of destruction in their wake. Desperate to avoid capture, they resorted to violence and intimidation to get what they needed. They robbed stores, stole vehicles, and even took hostages in their bid to stay one step ahead of the authorities.

One of the most chilling incidents during the crime spree involved the murder of a convenience store clerk who refused to comply with the escapees' demands. The clerk, who had been working the night shift, was shot and killed by Charles Thompson when he attempted to alert the authorities. The murder shocked the nation and intensified the urgency of the manhunt, as law enforcement agencies redoubled their efforts to capture the fugitives before they could commit further acts of violence.

The escapees also took several hostages during their time on the run, using them as human shields to deter law enforcement from attempting to apprehend them. In one particularly harrowing incident, the fugitives kidnapped a family from their home and forced them to accompany them as they continued their flight from justice. The family was eventually released unharmed, but the incident left them traumatized and underscored the dangerousness of the escapees.

Despite their efforts to evade capture, the escapees' luck eventually ran out. As the manhunt continued, law enforcement agencies began to close in on the fugitives, tracking their movements through a combination of tips from the public, surveillance footage, and forensic evidence. The escapees, who had become increasingly desperate as the net tightened around them, made a series of mistakes that ultimately led to their capture.

The Capture: Bringing the Fugitives to Justice

The end of the Oklahoma Prison Escape came when the escapees were finally cornered by law enforcement in a remote area of Texas. Acting on a tip from a local resident who had spotted the fugitives' vehicle, authorities surrounded the area and prepared to make their move. The escapees, realizing that they had been found, attempted to flee on foot, but they were quickly apprehended by law enforcement officers who had been lying in wait.

The capture of the escapees brought an end to the manhunt and a sense of relief to a nation that had been gripped by fear during the weeks-long search. The fugitives were taken into custody without further incident and were extradited back to Oklahoma to face justice for their crimes. The capture was widely covered in the media, with images of the escapees being led away in handcuffs broadcast on television screens across the country.

Following their capture, the escapees were tried and convicted for their roles in the escape and the crimes they had committed while on the run. Charles Thompson was sentenced to death for the murder of the convenience store clerk, while Randolph Dial received a life sentence for his involvement in the escape and other related crimes. Bobbi Parker, who had assisted in the escape, was also tried and convicted, receiving a lengthy prison sentence for her role in the conspiracy.

Aftermath and Legacy: The Impact of the Oklahoma Prison Escape

The Oklahoma Prison Escape had far-reaching consequences, both for the individuals involved and for the broader criminal justice system. The escape highlighted significant vulnerabilities within the Oklahoma State Penitentiary, prompting a series of investigations and reforms aimed at improving security and preventing future escapes. The prison's administration was criticized for its failure to prevent the escape, and several officials were either reassigned or resigned in the wake of the incident.

The escape also had a lasting impact on the families of the victims, particularly those who had lost loved ones during the crime spree. The murder of the convenience store clerk was a particularly tragic event, leaving his family devastated and seeking justice for his senseless death. The escapees' actions also left a lasting psychological scar on the hostages they had taken during their flight from the law, many of whom struggled with trauma long after the escape was over.

On a broader level, the Oklahoma Prison Escape served as a cautionary tale about the dangers of complacency within the prison system. It underscored the importance of maintaining strict security measures and highlighted the need for ongoing vigilance to prevent similar incidents from occurring in the future. The escape also sparked a national conversation about the treatment of prisoners and the conditions within American prisons, with some advocating for reforms to address the underlying issues that can lead to such desperate acts of violence.

Conclusion

The Oklahoma Prison Escape is a stark reminder of the lengths to which some individuals will go to regain their freedom and the chaos that can ensue when the system fails to contain them. The escape, which involved meticulous planning, violence, and a nationwide manhunt, captivated the nation and left a lasting impact on those involved. It also served as a wake-up call for the criminal justice system, prompting reforms and changes aimed at preventing similar incidents in the future. While the escapees were eventually brought to justice, the legacy of the Oklahoma Prison Escape continues to resonate, serving as a sobering reminder of the dangers that lurk within the walls of America's prisons.

Chapter 12: El Chapo's Escape

The story of Joaquín "El Chapo" Guzmán, one of the most infamous drug lords in history, is one of power, violence, and relentless pursuit of control over the global narcotics trade. However, among the many chapters of his criminal career, one of the most remarkable and audacious is his escape from a maximum-security prison in Mexico. El Chapo's escape from the Altiplano prison in 2015 is a tale of extraordinary planning, cunning, and the exploitation of systemic corruption within Mexico's penal and law enforcement systems. This detailed account delves into the background of El Chapo, the intricacies of his escape, the aftermath, and the broader implications of his breakout on both Mexican society and the international war on drugs.

The Man Behind the Myth: Joaquín "El Chapo" Guzmán

Joaquín Archivaldo Guzmán Loera, better known as El Chapo (which translates to "Shorty" due to his height of 5 feet 6 inches), was born on April 4, 1957, in La Tuna, a small village in the Mexican state of Sinaloa. Raised in a poor family, Guzmán's early life was marked by hardship and exposure to the drug trade, which had long been a part of the region's economy. By the late 1980s, Guzmán had risen through the ranks of the Sinaloa Cartel, a powerful drug trafficking organization, eventually becoming its leader.

Under El Chapo's leadership, the Sinaloa Cartel grew into one of the most powerful criminal organizations in the world. Known for his ruthless tactics and strategic acumen, Guzmán was responsible for overseeing the production, transportation, and distribution of vast quantities of cocaine, marijuana, heroin, and methamphetamine across international borders, particularly into the United States. His operations generated billions of dollars in revenue, and his influence extended far beyond Mexico's borders, making him one of the most wanted men in the world.

Guzmán's criminal empire was built on a foundation of violence, corruption, and intimidation. He maintained control over his operations through a network of loyal lieutenants, bribed officials, and armed enforcers who ensured that his orders were carried out and his rivals eliminated. Despite numerous attempts by law enforcement to capture him, El Chapo managed to evade capture for years, cementing his reputation as an elusive and cunning criminal mastermind.

The First Capture and Escape

El Chapo's first significant brush with the law came in 1993 when he was captured in Guatemala and extradited to Mexico, where he was sentenced to 20 years in prison for drug trafficking, bribery, and conspiracy. However, even behind bars, Guzmán continued to run his criminal empire, using bribes and his extensive network of contacts to maintain his influence.

In 2001, after spending eight years in a high-security prison in Puente Grande, Jalisco, Guzmán executed his first escape. The breakout was a masterclass in manipulation and corruption. Guzmán bribed prison officials, including guards and even the warden, to assist in his escape. On the day of his escape, he was smuggled out of the prison in a laundry cart, a method that became legendary in the annals of criminal history. His escape marked the beginning of another decade of dominance for the Sinaloa Cartel, during which Guzmán expanded his operations and became even more powerful.

The 2014 Capture: A Major Victory for Law Enforcement

El Chapo's freedom came to an end on February 22, 2014, when he was captured by Mexican authorities in a raid on a beachfront condominium in Mazatlán, Sinaloa. The operation, carried out by

Mexican Marines with support from U.S. intelligence agencies, was hailed as a significant victory in the fight against drug trafficking. Guzmán was promptly returned to prison, this time to the Altiplano maximum-security facility, located about 55 miles west of Mexico City.

The Altiplano prison, formally known as the Federal Social Readaptation Center No. 1, was considered one of the most secure prisons in Mexico. It was equipped with extensive surveillance systems, heavily fortified walls, and a large contingent of guards. Guzmán was placed under strict security measures, including 24-hour video surveillance and regular cell inspections. The Mexican government was determined to ensure that El Chapo would not escape again, given the embarrassment and damage to its credibility that his previous escape had caused.

Planning the Escape: A Masterpiece of Criminal Engineering

Despite the heightened security at Altiplano, El Chapo was not deterred. His mind was constantly at work, strategizing his next move. Unbeknownst to the authorities, Guzmán and his associates were meticulously planning another escape, one that would surpass his previous breakout in both audacity and complexity.

The plan hinged on a combination of inside help, external resources, and El Chapo's vast financial resources. Over the course of several months, his associates began work on a tunnel that would lead directly to Guzmán's cell. The tunnel was an engineering marvel, measuring nearly a mile long and equipped with lighting, ventilation, and even a modified motorcycle mounted on rails, which was used to transport dirt out of the tunnel and bring supplies in.

The tunnel began in a small, nondescript building in the town of Almoloya de Juárez, located near the Altiplano prison. From there, it snaked underground, passing beneath the prison's walls and security systems, before finally emerging beneath the floor of Guzmán's cell. The construction of the tunnel required immense precision, as it had to be aligned perfectly with the coordinates of Guzmán's cell, all while avoiding detection by the prison's surveillance systems.

To achieve this, Guzmán's associates relied on advanced technology, including GPS devices and construction equipment, as well as the expertise of engineers and tunnel diggers who had previously worked on the cartel's network of drug-smuggling tunnels along the U.S.-Mexico border. The entire operation was funded by the Sinaloa Cartel, with millions of dollars being funneled into the project to ensure its success.

The Escape: A Breathtaking Execution

On the evening of July 11, 2015, El Chapo put the escape plan into action. At around 8:52 p.m., Guzmán entered the shower area of his cell, which was one of the few blind spots in the prison's surveillance system. There, he lifted a trapdoor that had been hidden beneath the floor and descended into the tunnel that had been constructed specifically for his escape. Once inside the tunnel, Guzmán climbed onto the waiting motorcycle and sped through the underground passage, covering the nearly mile-long distance in a matter of minutes.

The tunnel led Guzmán to the building in Almoloya de Juárez, where his associates were waiting for him. From there, he was whisked away to a safe house, where he would remain hidden for the next several weeks. By the time prison officials realized that Guzmán was missing, he was already long gone, and a nationwide manhunt was launched to recapture him.

The escape was a devastating blow to the Mexican government, which had assured the public that Guzmán would not be able to escape from Altiplano. The incident exposed significant flaws in the country's prison system, particularly in terms of corruption and security. It also highlighted the immense power and influence that El Chapo and the Sinaloa Cartel wielded, both inside and outside of prison.

The Aftermath: A Global Manhunt

Following El Chapo's escape, Mexican authorities, with assistance from the United States, launched an intense manhunt to locate and recapture the fugitive drug lord. The search spanned across Mexico and extended into other countries, as law enforcement agencies worked around the clock to track down Guzmán and his associates. The Mexican government offered a substantial reward for information leading to his capture, and the escape became a top priority for both Mexican and U.S. law enforcement agencies.

As the manhunt intensified, Guzmán was forced to remain on the move, constantly changing locations to avoid detection. Despite his efforts to evade capture, law enforcement officials were able to track his movements through a combination of intelligence gathering, surveillance, and tips from informants. Guzmán's attempts to rebuild his criminal empire while on the run only served to draw more attention to his whereabouts.

In January 2016, just six months after his escape, El Chapo was finally recaptured by Mexican authorities. The operation that led to his capture was a carefully coordinated effort involving Mexican Marines, U.S. intelligence agencies, and local law enforcement. Guzmán was found hiding in a house in the city of Los Mochis, Sinaloa, after a shootout with Mexican Marines. He was taken into custody and promptly returned to Altiplano prison, but this time, the Mexican government made it clear that they would not take any chances.

Extradition to the United States and Final Justice

Following his recapture, the Mexican government faced immense pressure from the United States to extradite Guzmán, where he would face charges in multiple states for his role in leading the Sinaloa Cartel. The U.S. government argued that keeping Guzmán in Mexico would only increase the risk of another escape, given the corruption and weaknesses within the Mexican prison system.

In January 2017, after a lengthy legal process, El Chapo was extradited to the United States. He was flown to New York, where he would stand trial for a litany of charges, including drug trafficking, money laundering, and murder. The trial, which began in November 2018, was one of the most high-profile criminal cases in U.S. history, drawing extensive media coverage and public interest.

During the trial, prosecutors presented overwhelming evidence of Guzmán's crimes, including testimony from former cartel members, intercepted communications, and financial records. The trial painted a detailed picture of the inner workings of the Sinaloa Cartel and the violence and corruption that fueled its operations. After several months of testimony, Guzmán was found guilty on all counts and was sentenced to life in prison without the possibility of parole, plus 30 years.

El Chapo was subsequently sent to the United States Penitentiary Administrative Maximum Facility (ADX) in Florence, Colorado, often referred to as the "Alcatraz of the Rockies." The prison is known for its strict security measures and is considered one of the most secure facilities in the world, housing some of the most dangerous criminals. There, Guzmán would spend the rest of his life, isolated from the outside world and unable to orchestrate any further escapes.

The Legacy of El Chapo's Escape

El Chapo's 2015 escape from Altiplano prison remains one of the most audacious and sophisticated prison breaks in modern history. It highlighted the deep-seated corruption within the Mexican prison system and the challenges that law enforcement faces in dealing with powerful and resourceful criminals like Guzmán. The escape also underscored the global reach of the Sinaloa Cartel and the ongoing battle between drug traffickers and authorities.

While Guzmán's final capture and extradition to the United States marked the end of his reign as the leader of the Sinaloa Cartel, his legacy continues to influence the world of organized crime. The Sinaloa Cartel remains a dominant force in the global drug trade, and the power vacuum left by Guzmán's imprisonment has led to further violence and competition among rival factions.

Moreover, El Chapo's story has been immortalized in popular culture, with numerous books, documentaries, and films exploring his life and criminal exploits. His escape has become a symbol of both the cunning and ruthlessness of drug lords and the ongoing struggle to combat the influence of organized crime.

Conclusion

The escape of Joaquín "El Chapo" Guzmán from Altiplano prison in 2015 is a testament to the lengths that powerful criminals will go to regain their freedom and continue their illicit activities. It serves as a reminder of the challenges that law enforcement faces in dealing with organized crime and the importance of vigilance and integrity within the criminal justice system. While El Chapo's story is one of crime and violence, it also offers valuable lessons about the consequences of corruption and the need for international cooperation in the fight against drug trafficking.

Chapter 13: Parkhurst Prison Escape

The Parkhurst Prison escape of 1995 remains one of the most notorious jailbreaks in British history. Located on the Isle of Wight, Parkhurst Prison was once considered one of the most secure prisons in the United Kingdom, often referred to as Britain's "Alcatraz." The escape, executed by three dangerous inmates, highlighted significant flaws in the prison system and shocked the nation. This detailed account delves into the history of Parkhurst Prison, the circumstances leading to the escape, the intricacies of the breakout, the subsequent manhunt, and the broader implications for the British penal system.

The History and Notoriety of Parkhurst Prison

Parkhurst Prison, established in 1863, is one of the oldest prisons in the United Kingdom. Located on the Isle of Wight, an island off the southern coast of England, Parkhurst was originally built as a military hospital but was soon converted into a prison. Over the years, it gained a reputation for housing some of the country's most dangerous and violent criminals, including murderers, rapists, and armed robbers. Due to the high-profile nature of many of its inmates, the prison was often compared to the infamous Alcatraz in the United States.

Parkhurst was classified as a Category A prison, meaning it was designed to hold the most high-risk prisoners who posed a severe threat to public safety. The prison was known for its strict security measures, including high walls, extensive surveillance, and a large staff of guards. Inmates were kept under constant watch, and any attempt at escape was considered almost impossible. However, despite its reputation for security, Parkhurst had a history of disturbances, including riots, attacks on staff, and even a few escape attempts, though none were as successful or as shocking as the one that occurred in January 1995.

The Inmates: Dangerous Men Behind Bars

The escape of January 1995 involved three inmates: Keith Rose, Matthew Williams, and Andrew Rodger. All three men were serving lengthy sentences for violent crimes, and their backgrounds made them particularly dangerous.

- **Keith Rose**: Rose was a skilled engineer with a background in aircraft maintenance. He was serving a life sentence for the brutal murder of an elderly woman during a robbery. Rose was known for his intelligence and technical skills, which he would later use to orchestrate the escape.
- **Matthew Williams**: Williams was serving a life sentence for a string of violent armed robberies. He had a history of criminal behavior dating back to his youth and was considered highly dangerous. Williams was also known for his physical strength and ability to intimidate others.
- **Andrew Rodger**: Rodger was serving a long sentence for attempted murder and other violent offenses. He had a history of mental health issues and had been involved in numerous violent incidents both in and out of prison. Rodger was regarded as highly unpredictable and volatile.

The three men had formed a close bond during their time in Parkhurst, and together, they began to plot their escape. They were well aware of the challenges they faced in breaking out of one of the most secure prisons in the country, but they were determined to succeed.

Planning the Escape: A Plot in the Making

The planning of the Parkhurst escape was a meticulous and highly organized operation that took months to prepare. The three inmates used their individual skills and knowledge to devise a plan that would exploit the weaknesses in the prison's security system.

- **Gathering Materials and Tools**

One of the key elements of the escape was the acquisition of materials and tools needed to break out. Keith Rose, with his background in engineering, took the lead in this aspect of the plan. Over several months, Rose managed to collect various tools and materials, including hacksaw blades, screwdrivers, wire cutters, and even a homemade ladder. These items were smuggled into the prison or obtained from the prison's workshops, where Rose had access to equipment as part of his work duties.

- **Reconnaissance and Identifying Weaknesses**

The inmates conducted extensive reconnaissance of the prison's layout, focusing on identifying potential weaknesses in the security system. They studied the prison's routine, including the movements of guards, the timing of patrols, and the locations of surveillance cameras. Through careful observation, they identified a section of the prison wall that was less heavily monitored and would be their target for the escape.

- **Creating the Plan**

The plan involved several key steps: cutting through the bars of their cells, navigating the prison's corridors without being detected, cutting through the perimeter fence, and finally scaling the prison wall using the homemade ladder. The timing of the escape was crucial, as they needed to avoid detection by guards and cameras at all costs. The inmates decided to carry out the escape during the early hours of the morning when the prison was at its quietest and the guards were less vigilant.

- **The Role of Disguises**

To further enhance their chances of success, the inmates created disguises to blend in with the prison staff. They fashioned makeshift uniforms and used materials like paint and fabric to create badges and insignia that would make them look like maintenance workers or guards. The disguises were intended to give them the cover they needed to move around the prison without raising suspicion.

The Escape: A Daring Breakout

On the night of January 3, 1995, the inmates put their plan into action. The escape was a complex and dangerous operation that required precision and nerves of steel.

- **Breaking Out of the Cells**

The first step in the escape was to break out of their cells without being detected. Using the hacksaw blades they had smuggled into the prison, the inmates carefully cut through the bars of their cells. This was a slow and painstaking process that took several hours, as they had to work quietly to avoid alerting the guards. Once the bars were cut, they waited for the right moment to exit their cells.

- **Navigating the Prison Corridors**

After escaping their cells, the inmates navigated the prison's corridors, moving cautiously to avoid detection by guards and cameras. They relied on their disguises and knowledge of the prison's layout to move undetected. At one point, they had to disable a security camera by covering it with a piece of cloth, a risky maneuver that could have exposed their plan.

- **Cutting Through the Fence**

The next step involved cutting through the prison's perimeter fence. Using the wire cutters they had obtained; the inmates made a hole in the fence large enough for them to crawl through. This was another critical moment in the escape, as the fence was one of the main barriers between them and freedom.

- **Scaling the Wall**

The final and most dangerous part of the escape was scaling the prison wall. The inmates used the homemade ladder, which Rose had meticulously constructed, to climb over the wall. The wall was over 20 feet high, and the climb was treacherous, but the inmates managed to make it over without being detected.

- **Fleeing the Scene**

Once outside the prison, the inmates fled into the surrounding countryside. They had planned their escape route in advance and knew exactly where to go to avoid capture. The plan was to head to the mainland, where they hoped to disappear into the population.

The Manhunt: A Nation on High Alert

The escape was discovered early the next morning when guards conducting routine checks found the empty cells and the cut bars. The alarm was raised immediately, and a massive manhunt was launched to recapture the fugitives. The escape made headlines across the United Kingdom, and the public was warned that three dangerous criminals were on the loose.

- **Law Enforcement Response**

The response from law enforcement was swift and intense. Hundreds of police officers were deployed to search the Isle of Wight and the surrounding areas. Roadblocks were set up, and ferries and boats leaving the island were closely monitored. The police also issued a nationwide alert, as it was believed that the fugitives might try to flee the country.

- **Media Coverage**

The escape received extensive media coverage, with news outlets providing regular updates on the search for the fugitives. The public was urged to remain vigilant and report any sightings of the escaped prisoners. The media also delved into the backgrounds of the three men, highlighting their violent pasts and the potential danger they posed to society.

- **The Capture**

Despite their efforts to evade capture, the fugitives were eventually caught. The first to be apprehended was Andrew Rodger, who was found hiding in a shed near the prison just a few days after the escape. Matthew Williams was captured shortly thereafter in a nearby town. The last to be caught was Keith Rose, who managed to evade capture for several days but was eventually found hiding in a barn. The escapees were returned to Parkhurst Prison under even tighter security, and their brief taste of freedom was brought to an abrupt end.

The Aftermath: A Wake-Up Call for the British Penal System

The Parkhurst escape had far-reaching consequences for the British penal system. It exposed significant flaws in the security measures at one of the country's most secure prisons and raised serious questions about the management and oversight of dangerous inmates.

- **Security Reforms**

In the wake of the escape, a thorough investigation was conducted to determine how the inmates had managed to break out. The investigation revealed several lapses in security, including inadequate surveillance, poor coordination among prison staff, and a lack of proper checks on the inmates' activities. As a result, the British government implemented a series of security reforms across the prison system, including the installation of additional cameras, improved training for prison staff, and stricter controls on access to tools and materials.

- **Public Outcry and Political Fallout**

The escape also led to a public outcry and political fallout. The incident was widely seen as an embarrassment for the British government and a failure of the criminal justice system. The Home Secretary at the time faced intense criticism and was forced to address the issue in Parliament. The escape became a rallying point for calls to reform the prison system and improve public safety.

- **Impact on Inmates**

For the inmates involved in the escape, the consequences were severe. All three men were given additional sentences for their escape attempts, and their privileges within the prison were revoked. They were placed under even stricter confinement, with limited access to other inmates and close monitoring by prison staff.

Conclusion: A Legendary Escape

The Parkhurst Prison escape of 1995 remains one of the most infamous jailbreaks in British history. It was a daring and meticulously planned operation that exposed significant weaknesses in what was supposed to be one of the most secure prisons in the country. The escape highlighted the ingenuity and determination of the inmates involved, as well as the ongoing challenges faced by the criminal justice system in containing and managing dangerous offenders.

The legacy of the Parkhurst escape continues to be felt in the British penal system, where security measures have been tightened and lessons have been learned from the failures that allowed the escape to occur. The incident serves as a reminder of the risks inherent in managing high-risk prisoners and the importance of constant vigilance and improvement in prison security.

Chapter 14: Helicopter Jailbreak

Helicopter jailbreaks stand out as some of the most audacious and cinematic prison escapes in history. Unlike typical methods of digging tunnels or smuggling in contraband tools, helicopter escapes involve the use of airborne vehicles, allowing prisoners to bypass the formidable walls, barbed wire, and security measures that traditional escapes must overcome. These escapes are rare due to the complex logistics and coordination required, but they are often successful due to their speed and the element of surprise. Helicopter jailbreaks have captured the imagination of the public and are the subject of numerous books, documentaries, and even films. This form of escape showcases the lengths to which some prisoners will go to regain their freedom and the intricate planning that such operations require.

The Concept of Helicopter Jailbreaks

A helicopter jailbreak involves the use of a helicopter, usually hijacked or coerced, to break a prisoner out of a facility. The idea is deceptively simple: a helicopter lands in or near the prison yard, picks up the prisoner, and flies off before the authorities can respond. However, the execution of this idea is incredibly complex and requires meticulous planning. A successful helicopter jailbreak necessitates precise timing, a skilled pilot, and often, the involvement of outside accomplices who can commandeer the helicopter and ensure its safe landing and departure. The daring nature of these escapes makes them particularly dangerous, both for the escapees and the civilians who may be involved.

The History of Helicopter Jailbreaks

The first recorded helicopter jailbreak took place in France in 1971 when a convicted bank robber named Joannès "Jo" Cassou was broken out of a prison in Lyon. His associates hijacked a helicopter and forced the pilot to land in the prison courtyard. Cassou climbed aboard, and they flew away, marking the beginning of what would become a trend in certain parts of the world. France, in particular, has a long history of helicopter jailbreaks, with several high-profile escapes occurring in the years since.

One of the most famous cases involved the notorious French criminal Michel Vaujour. In 1986, Vaujour, serving time for armed robbery, escaped from a prison in Paris with the help of his wife, Nadine. Nadine had taken helicopter flying lessons under a false name and, on the day of the escape, she rented a helicopter, flew it to the prison, and picked up her husband. The escape was successful, although Vaujour was recaptured a few months later.

Another significant helicopter jailbreak occurred in 2001 when a group of prisoners in the maximum-security prison of Korydallos in Greece broke out with the help of a hijacked helicopter. Among the escapees was Vassilis Paleokostas, a notorious Greek criminal who would later be involved in another helicopter jailbreak in 2009, making him one of the most famous figures associated with this escape method.

Notable Helicopter Jailbreaks

- **Michel Vaujour's 1986 Escape**

Michel Vaujour's escape from the La Santé Prison in Paris is one of the most remarkable helicopter jailbreaks in history. Vaujour was a career criminal with a reputation for violence and ingenuity. While incarcerated, he plotted his escape with his wife, Nadine. She trained for months to fly a helicopter, eventually gaining enough skill to rent one under an alias. On May 26, 1986, Nadine flew the helicopter over the prison yard, where Michel had managed to get access to the roof. As guards watched in astonishment, Michel climbed aboard, and the helicopter flew off. The couple evaded capture for a short time, but Michel was eventually shot and wounded in a confrontation with police, leading to his recapture.

- **Vassilis Paleokostas' Escapes**

Vassilis Paleokostas, often referred to as the "Greek Robin Hood," became infamous for his helicopter escapes. The first occurred in 2006 when he and an accomplice used a helicopter to escape from Korydallos Prison in Athens. The helicopter landed in the prison yard, and despite heavy security, Paleokostas and his fellow escapee managed to board it and fly to freedom. Three years later, in 2009, Paleokostas repeated the feat, escaping once again from the same prison using another helicopter. His escapes were seen as a major embarrassment for the Greek authorities, and Paleokostas became a folk hero in some circles due to his reputation for stealing from the rich and helping the poor.

- **Pascal Payet's Escapes**

Pascal Payet, a French criminal known for his involvement in several high-profile robberies, also became famous for his helicopter escapes. In 2001, Payet escaped from Luynes Prison in southern France after his associates hijacked a helicopter and flew it into the prison yard. After being recaptured, Payet organized another helicopter escape in 2003, but this time, he was not the one escaping. Instead, he helped orchestrate the escape of three other inmates from the same prison. Payet was eventually recaptured, but in 2007, he managed to escape yet again, this time from Grasse Prison, using a helicopter. Payet's repeated escapes highlighted the vulnerabilities in the French prison system and led to increased security measures.

- **Antonio Ferrara's Escape**

In 2003, Italian criminal Antonio Ferrara, known for his involvement in a series of bank robberies, escaped from Fresnes Prison near Paris in another dramatic helicopter jailbreak. Ferrara's accomplices hijacked a helicopter and flew it to the prison, where they used explosives to break through the prison walls and allow Ferrara to escape. The escape was meticulously planned, with the helicopter pilot being coerced into participating. Ferrara's escape sparked a massive manhunt, and he was eventually recaptured, but his jailbreak remains one of the most notorious in French history.

Planning and Execution: The Anatomy of a Helicopter Jailbreak

Helicopter jailbreaks require an extraordinary level of planning and coordination. The first step usually involves securing a helicopter, which is often done through hijacking or coercing a pilot into cooperating. In some cases, the escapees or their accomplices may even undergo pilot training to ensure the operation goes smoothly. The choice of helicopter is also crucial, as it needs to be fast, agile, and capable of landing in tight spaces such as prison courtyards.

The timing of the escape is another critical factor. Helicopter jailbreaks typically occur during periods when prison security is less vigilant, such as during shift changes or when prisoners are allowed outside for exercise. The escapees must also coordinate with accomplices outside the prison to ensure that the helicopter arrives at the right moment.

Communication between the prisoners and their outside accomplices is essential for the success of a helicopter jailbreak. This communication is often carried out using contraband cell phones, smuggled messages, or even code words passed through visitors or legal representatives. The escapees must be in the right place at the right time, ready to board the helicopter as soon as it arrives.

Once the helicopter lands, the prisoners must move quickly to avoid detection or interception by prison guards. In some cases, the escapees may use weapons or explosives to fend off security personnel and ensure a swift departure. The helicopter then flies to a predetermined location where the prisoners can safely disembark and make their way to a hideout or rendezvous point with further transportation.

The Risks and Challenges of Helicopter Jailbreaks

While helicopter jailbreaks may seem like an ideal escape method, they come with significant risks and challenges. One of the biggest dangers is the potential for violence, as guards may open fire on the helicopter or the escapees. In some cases, helicopters have been shot down, leading to fatal crashes. Additionally, the involvement of civilians, such as pilots, adds another layer of complexity and moral ambiguity to the escape. These individuals may be unwilling participants, forced to aid in the escape under duress.

Another challenge is the difficulty of evading capture after the escape. While helicopters provide a fast and dramatic means of leaving the prison, they are also highly visible and can be tracked by law enforcement. Escapees must quickly transition to other forms of transportation or hideouts to avoid being recaptured.

The planning of a helicopter jailbreak also requires a significant amount of resources, including money, weapons, and logistical support. The escapees must be able to trust their accomplices, as any betrayal or failure in the plan can lead to disaster. Moreover, once an escape occurs, the authorities are likely to increase security measures at other prisons, making future helicopter jailbreaks even more difficult to pull off.

Legal and Security Implications

Helicopter jailbreaks have profound legal and security implications. For prison authorities, these escapes highlight weaknesses in their security systems and often lead to widespread criticism and calls for reform. In response to helicopter jailbreaks, many prisons have implemented new security measures, such as the installation of anti-aircraft nets or wire, restricted airspace over prison facilities, and increased surveillance of potential accomplices on the outside.

For the legal system, helicopter jailbreaks pose challenges in terms of prosecution and sentencing. Escapees who are recaptured often face additional charges, and those who assisted in the escape can be prosecuted for aiding and abetting. The high-profile nature of these escapes also means that recaptured prisoners are often placed under much stricter security conditions, with limited opportunities for further escape attempts.

Conclusion

Helicopter jailbreaks are some of the most daring and ingenious prison escapes in history. While they are rare due to the complexity and risks involved, they capture the imagination of the public and have become legendary in criminal folklore. The cases of Michel Vaujour, Vassilis Paleokostas, Pascal Payet, and others demonstrate the lengths to which some prisoners will go to regain their freedom, and the challenges that law enforcement faces in preventing such escapes. Helicopter jailbreaks serve as a reminder of the ongoing cat-and-mouse game between criminals and authorities and the ever-evolving tactics used on both sides.

Chapter 15: Gerald Chapman

Gerald Chapman is a name that looms large in the annals of American criminal history. Born in the late 19th century, Chapman became infamous during the early 20th century as one of the nation's most notorious criminals, earning the dubious distinction of being America's first "Public Enemy No. 1." His life was a complex tapestry of audacious crimes, dramatic escapes, and a relentless pursuit by law enforcement, culminating in a trial and execution that captivated the nation. Gerald Chapman's story is not just one of crime, but also one of transformation—from a small-time crook to a master thief, and ultimately, a symbol of the lawlessness that plagued America during the Prohibition era.

Early Life: From Ordinary Beginnings to Criminal Aspirations

Gerald Chapman was born on August 8, 1887, in Brooklyn, New York. His early life was relatively unremarkable, marked by the ordinary challenges of a working-class family in New York City. There is little in the historical record to suggest that Chapman showed any signs of the criminal genius he would later become. However, like many young men of his time, Chapman found himself drawn into a life of crime, lured by the promise of quick money and excitement.

Chapman's early criminal activities were relatively small-time. He started with petty thefts and gradually escalated to more serious crimes. By his early twenties, he had become a proficient thief, known for his cunning and ability to evade capture. However, it was his association with another notorious criminal, George "Dutch" Anderson, that would propel him into the upper echelons of American crime.

The Rise of a Master Criminal: The Chapman-Anderson Gang

Chapman's partnership with Dutch Anderson proved to be a turning point in his criminal career. Anderson, a well-educated man with a penchant for elaborate schemes, recognized Chapman's talents and saw in him a kindred spirit. Together, they formed the Chapman-Anderson Gang, a criminal enterprise that specialized in high-profile heists and robberies.

The gang's most famous exploit came in 1921, when they orchestrated what was, at the time, the largest cash robbery in American history. On October 24, 1921, Chapman, Anderson, and their associates held up a U.S. Mail truck in New York City, making off with $2.4 million in cash, bonds, and securities—a staggering sum equivalent to over $35 million today. The heist was a meticulously planned operation that demonstrated Chapman's intelligence, nerve, and organizational skills. It also marked him as a criminal of national significance.

The robbery sent shockwaves through the country, and law enforcement agencies launched a massive manhunt to apprehend the culprits. Despite the pressure, Chapman managed to evade capture for several months, moving from city to city and living under assumed identities. His ability to stay one step ahead of the authorities only added to his growing legend.

Capture and Incarceration: The End of the Road?

Chapman's luck eventually ran out in January 1922 when he was arrested in New York City. At the time of his capture, he was found with a large cache of weapons and stolen goods, further solidifying his reputation as a dangerous criminal. He was charged with multiple offenses, including the infamous mail truck robbery, and was sentenced to 25 years in prison at the federal penitentiary in Atlanta, Georgia.

For many criminals, a 25-year sentence would have marked the end of their story, but not for Gerald Chapman. While incarcerated, he continued to plot and scheme, determined not to spend the rest of his life behind bars. Chapman's time in prison only served to hone his criminal instincts and further his notoriety.

The Daring Escape from Atlanta Penitentiary

In 1923, Chapman made headlines once again with a daring escape from the Atlanta Federal Penitentiary. His escape was nothing short of audacious and added another layer to his already infamous reputation. Chapman, along with two other inmates, managed to overpower guards and make their way out of the high-security facility. The escape was meticulously planned, with Chapman using his cunning and resourcefulness to outwit the prison authorities.

The escape caused a national sensation, with newspapers across the country reporting on the manhunt for Chapman. Law enforcement agencies, already embarrassed by Chapman's successful evasion after the mail truck robbery, were now under intense pressure to recapture him. The public, meanwhile, was both horrified and fascinated by the story of the escaped convict, who had now become a household name.

Life on the Run: Chapman's Elusive Years

After his escape from the Atlanta Penitentiary, Chapman embarked on a life as a fugitive. He moved frequently, never staying in one place for too long, and continued to engage in criminal activities to fund his life on the run. His ability to evade capture was remarkable, and he became a master of disguise and deception, often altering his appearance and using false identities to throw off the authorities.

During this period, Chapman committed several more crimes, including robberies and burglaries. His criminal exploits were covered extensively in the media, and his legend grew with each passing day. Despite the best efforts of law enforcement, Chapman remained at large, a ghostly figure who seemed always to be one step ahead of his pursuers.

Chapman was not without his moments of near capture. On several occasions, he narrowly escaped the clutches of the law, often through sheer luck or quick thinking. These close calls only added to his mystique, making him a symbol of defiance against the authorities.

The Downfall: The Killing of Officer James Skelly

Chapman's life on the run came to a tragic and violent end in 1924. On October 12, 1924, in New Britain, Connecticut, Chapman was involved in a confrontation that would seal his fate. During an attempted robbery, he encountered Police Officer James Skelly. In the ensuing struggle, Chapman shot and killed Skelly, a crime that would mark the beginning of the end for America's first "Public Enemy No. 1."

The murder of a police officer significantly escalated the manhunt for Chapman. Killing a law enforcement officer was a crime that carried severe consequences, and the authorities were now more determined than ever to bring Chapman to justice. The killing of Officer Skelly also turned public opinion against Chapman, who had previously been seen by some as a sort of anti-hero. Now, he was viewed as a cold-blooded killer who needed to be stopped at all costs.

Capture and Trial: The Fall of a Criminal Mastermind

Gerald Chapman's luck finally ran out in January 1925 when he was apprehended in Muncie, Indiana. His capture was a major victory for law enforcement, and it marked the end of one of the most extensive manhunts in American history. Chapman's arrest was front-page news, and the public followed every detail of his case with intense interest.

Chapman's trial for the murder of Officer Skelly was a highly publicized affair. Held in Hartford, Connecticut, the trial attracted widespread media attention and was seen as a test of the criminal justice system's ability to bring a notorious criminal to justice. Chapman, ever the showman, conducted himself with a mixture of arrogance and defiance during the proceedings, but the evidence against him was overwhelming.

In the end, Gerald Chapman was found guilty of murder and sentenced to death. Despite several appeals and efforts to secure a reprieve, the sentence was upheld, and Chapman's fate was sealed. The trial and sentencing marked the final chapter in the life of a man who had spent years defying the law and living outside the boundaries of society.

Execution: The End of the Line

On April 6, 1926, Gerald Chapman was executed by hanging at the Connecticut State Prison in Wethersfield. His execution was a significant event, drawing large crowds of onlookers and extensive media coverage. For many, Chapman's execution represented the triumph of law and order over lawlessness, a fitting end for a man who had terrorized the country for years.

Chapman remained defiant to the end, showing little remorse for his actions. His final words reportedly expressed his belief that he had been treated unfairly by the legal system, a sentiment that contrasted sharply with the public's view of him as a dangerous criminal who had finally gotten what he deserved.

Legacy: Gerald Chapman in History and Popular Culture

Gerald Chapman's legacy is a complex one. On one hand, he is remembered as one of America's most notorious criminals, a man who committed heinous crimes and showed little regard for the law or human life. His designation as the nation's first "Public Enemy No. 1" set the stage for future criminals who would receive the same label, including infamous figures like John Dillinger and Al Capone.

On the other hand, Chapman's life and crimes have become the stuff of legend, with his daring escapes, elaborate heists, and ability to evade capture capturing the public's imagination. His story has been recounted in numerous books, documentaries, and even films, making him a larger-than-life figure in American criminal history.

Chapman's influence can also be seen in the way law enforcement agencies approach high-profile criminals. His ability to outwit the authorities for so long highlighted the need for better coordination between different law enforcement bodies and more sophisticated methods of tracking and apprehending fugitives. In this sense, Chapman's criminal career had a lasting impact on the evolution of law enforcement in the United States.

Conclusion

Gerald Chapman's life was a testament to the extremes of human behavior—both in terms of his criminal exploits and the relentless pursuit by law enforcement to bring him to justice. From his humble beginnings in Brooklyn to his rise as America's most wanted man, Chapman's story is one of ambition, audacity, and ultimately, downfall. His legacy, while tarnished by his violent crimes, continues to intrigue and captivate those who study the history of crime in America. Gerald Chapman may have been a criminal, but his life and actions left an indelible mark on the nation's consciousness, forever cementing his place in the pantheon of American outlaws.

Chapter 16: Texas Seven

The story of the "Texas Seven" is one of the most dramatic and infamous prison escapes in modern American history. It involves a group of seven inmates who, in December 2000, executed a meticulously planned and daring breakout from a maximum-security prison in Texas. Their escape led to one of the largest and most intense manhunts in the United States, capturing the nation's attention for weeks. The Texas Seven were not just ordinary prisoners; they were dangerous criminals, convicted of serious crimes, and their escape led to further violence, including the murder of a police officer. This incident exposed flaws in the prison system, challenged law enforcement, and ultimately led to a dramatic and tragic conclusion. The saga of the Texas Seven is a tale of desperation, cunning, and the relentless pursuit of justice.

The Background: Who Were the Texas Seven?

The group known as the Texas Seven consisted of seven inmates, each with a history of violent crime, who were serving long sentences at the John B. Connally Unit, a maximum-security prison located near Kenedy, Texas. The inmates were:

1. **George Rivas** - The ringleader of the group, Rivas was serving a life sentence for aggravated robbery. A former Army reservist, Rivas was known for his intelligence and leadership abilities, which he used to orchestrate the escape plan.

2. **Joseph Garcia** - Garcia was serving a 50-year sentence for murder. He had a reputation for being tough and was considered one of the more dangerous members of the group.

3. **Randy Halprin** - Convicted of beating an infant, Halprin was serving a 30-year sentence. Despite his violent crime, Halprin was one of the younger and less experienced members of the

group.

4. **Larry Harper** - Serving 50 years for aggravated sexual assault, Harper was a hardened criminal with little hope of release.
5. **Donald Newbury** - Newbury was serving a 99-year sentence for robbery. Like Rivas, he was intelligent and resourceful, playing a key role in the escape.
6. **Patrick Murphy Jr.** - Murphy was serving a 50-year sentence for aggravated sexual assault. He was known for his quiet demeanor but was fully committed to the escape plan.
7. **Michael Rodriguez** - Rodriguez was serving life for hiring a hitman to murder his wife. He was a wealthy man who used his resources to help finance the escape.

These men, each with little hope of ever being released from prison, formed a bond based on their shared desperation and determination to escape. Together, they devised a plan that would exploit weaknesses in the prison's security system and allow them to make their break for freedom.

The Escape: A Bold and Calculated Plan

The escape from the John B. Connally Unit on December 13, 2000, was a meticulously planned and executed operation. The Texas Seven took advantage of several factors, including understaffing, complacency among prison guards, and their own cunning and ruthlessness.

The plan began with the group gaining control of the prison maintenance shop, where they were assigned to work. Over several days, they carefully studied the routines of the guards and identified vulnerabilities in the prison's security. On the day of the escape, they overpowered and restrained several prison employees, including civilian maintenance workers and correctional officers. The group used the employees' uniforms, identification badges, and radios to impersonate guards and create confusion within the prison.

Once they had control of the maintenance shop, the Texas Seven split into two groups. One group stayed behind to guard the hostages, while the other began making their way through the prison, cutting phone lines and disabling the security system to prevent any alarms from being triggered. Using the stolen uniforms and IDs, they moved through the prison without arousing suspicion.

Their ultimate goal was the prison's back gate, where deliveries were made. They hijacked a prison truck and used it to breach the gate, driving out of the facility before anyone realized what had happened. The entire operation took just a few hours, and by the time the alarm was raised, the Texas Seven were already on the road, heading for their new lives as fugitives.

Life on the Run: Robbery and Murder

After their escape, the Texas Seven embarked on a crime spree to finance their life on the run. Their first target was a sporting goods store in Irving, Texas, which they robbed on Christmas Eve, 2000. The robbery was well-planned, and the group made off with guns, ammunition, clothing, and cash. However, the robbery took a tragic turn when they encountered Officer Aubrey Hawkins, a 29-year-old police officer who responded to the scene.

The Texas Seven ambushed Hawkins, shooting him multiple times and then running him over with their vehicle to ensure he was dead. The murder of Officer Hawkins shocked the nation and intensified the manhunt for the fugitives. The killing marked a turning point in the saga of the Texas Seven, transforming them from escapees to cold-blooded killers and solidifying their place as some of the most wanted men in America.

The Nationwide Manhunt: Law Enforcement on High Alert

The murder of Officer Hawkins set off one of the largest manhunts in U.S. history. Law enforcement agencies across the country were mobilized to capture the Texas Seven, and the FBI placed the fugitives on their Ten Most Wanted list. The escapees' faces were plastered on wanted posters, and their story was broadcast on television and radio stations nationwide. A reward of $500,000 was offered for information leading to their capture, and the public was urged to be vigilant.

Despite the intense pressure, the Texas Seven managed to evade capture for several weeks. They traveled across the country, changing vehicles and using stolen identities to avoid detection. At one point, they even spent time in a Colorado RV park, blending in with other vacationers and maintaining a low profile.

However, their luck began to run out in January 2001, when the television show "America's Most Wanted" aired a segment about the escape. A tip from a viewer led authorities to the Texas Seven's hideout in Woodland Park, Colorado. The manhunt culminated in a dramatic showdown, as law enforcement surrounded the fugitives' RV park and prepared to bring them in.

The Capture: A Violent and Tragic End

The capture of the Texas Seven was marked by violence and tragedy. On January 21, 2001, law enforcement agents, acting on the tip from "America's Most Wanted," descended on the RV park where the fugitives were hiding. Realizing they had been found, the Texas Seven prepared for a final standoff.

One of the fugitives, Larry Harper, chose not to surrender. Rather than face the possibility of life in prison or execution, Harper committed suicide, shooting himself in the chest as law enforcement closed in. The remaining six fugitives eventually surrendered after a tense standoff, bringing an end to their weeks-long run from justice.

The capture of the Texas Seven was a major victory for law enforcement, but it came at a heavy cost. The murder of Officer Aubrey Hawkins cast a long shadow over the case, and the escapees were now facing not only their original sentences but also the possibility of the death penalty for their involvement in the killing.

The Trials: Justice for the Texas Seven

Following their capture, the surviving members of the Texas Seven were extradited to Texas to stand trial for their crimes. The state of Texas sought the death penalty for all six of the remaining fugitives, citing the heinous nature of their crimes, particularly the murder of Officer Hawkins.

The trials were high-profile affairs, with intense media coverage and public interest. The prosecution presented a compelling case, detailing the group's escape, their crime spree, and the brutal murder of Officer Hawkins. Defense attorneys argued that their clients had been desperate men with little hope of ever being released from prison, but the jury was unmoved.

In 2003, the first of the Texas Seven, Michael Rodriguez, was sentenced to death. Over the next few years, the remaining five members—George Rivas, Joseph Garcia, Randy Halprin, Donald Newbury, and Patrick Murphy—were also sentenced to death. The convictions and sentences were upheld on appeal, and the Texas Seven's fate was sealed.

Executions and Appeals: The Final Chapter

The executions of the Texas Seven began in 2008, when Michael Rodriguez was put to death by lethal injection. Rodriguez had chosen to forgo further appeals and accepted his fate, expressing remorse for his crimes before his execution. His death marked the beginning of the end for the Texas Seven.

In 2011, George Rivas, the ringleader of the group, was executed. Rivas had shown no remorse during his trial but offered a brief apology to the Hawkins family before his execution. His death was followed by the executions of Donald Newbury in 2015, Joseph Garcia in 2018, and Patrick Murphy in 2019.

Randy Halprin, the last surviving member of the Texas Seven, has had his execution delayed due to ongoing legal battles. His case has drawn attention because of allegations of judicial bias during his trial. Halprin continues to fight his death sentence, but the legacy of the Texas Seven remains one of violence, desperation, and ultimately, justice.

Legacy: Lessons from the Texas Seven

The story of the Texas Seven is a stark reminder of the dangers posed by determined and desperate criminals. Their escape from the John B. Connally Unit exposed weaknesses in the prison system and led to increased scrutiny of security measures in Texas prisons. The incident also highlighted the challenges faced by law enforcement in tracking down and capturing dangerous fugitives, particularly when they are willing to use violence to achieve their goals.

The Texas Seven case also had a profound impact on the families of the victims, particularly the family of Officer Aubrey Hawkins. His murder was a senseless act of violence that left a lasting scar on the community and served as a tragic reminder of the risks faced by law enforcement officers every day.

In the years since the escape and subsequent manhunt, the Texas Seven have become a symbol of the dark side of human nature—of what can happen when individuals are pushed to the brink and choose to defy the law in the most extreme ways. Their story has been recounted in books, documentaries, and television programs, serving as both a cautionary tale and a testament to the resilience of those who pursue justice, no matter the cost.

Conclusion

The saga of the Texas Seven is a tale of audacity, violence, and the relentless pursuit of freedom at any cost. Their escape and subsequent crimes shocked the nation and led to a manhunt that captivated the public's imagination. While their story ended in capture, trials, and executions, the legacy of the Texas Seven continues to resonate as a powerful reminder of the dangers posed by those who are willing to stop at nothing to achieve their goals. The case serves as a testament to the bravery of law enforcement officers like Aubrey Hawkins and the enduring pursuit of justice in the face of even the most formidable challenges.

Chapter 17: Escape from Pretoria

The "Escape from Pretoria" stands as one of the most remarkable prison breaks in history, primarily because it wasn't orchestrated by hardened criminals but by political prisoners fighting against an oppressive regime. The story of Tim Jenkin and Stephen Lee, two white South Africans imprisoned for their anti-apartheid activism, is a testament to courage, ingenuity, and the unbreakable spirit of resistance. Their escape from Pretoria Central Prison in 1979 became a symbol of defiance against the apartheid regime and showcased the lengths to which individuals would go in the pursuit of justice and freedom. This escape, which involved meticulous planning, handcrafted wooden keys, and nerves of steel, is not only a thrilling tale but also a powerful reminder of the human capacity to resist injustice.

The Context: Apartheid in South Africa

To fully understand the significance of the "Escape from Pretoria," it is essential to grasp the political environment in which it took place. South Africa in the 1970s was a country deeply divided by apartheid, a system of institutionalized racial segregation and discrimination that oppressed the non-white majority and privileged the white minority. The apartheid regime, led by the National Party, enforced strict racial laws that governed every aspect of life, from where people could live and work to who they could marry.

The African National Congress (ANC), along with other anti-apartheid movements, fought tirelessly against this system, often at great personal risk. As the struggle intensified, the South African government cracked down on dissent, imprisoning activists, banning political organizations, and using violence to maintain control. It was in this highly charged atmosphere that Tim Jenkin and Stephen Lee, both members of the ANC, were arrested and imprisoned for their activism.

Tim Jenkin and Stephen Lee: The Freedom Fighters

Tim Jenkin and Stephen Lee were not your typical criminals. They were political activists committed to the fight against apartheid. Born into privileged white families, both men could have led comfortable lives under the apartheid system, but they chose a different path. They rejected the racist policies of the government and aligned themselves with the ANC, becoming involved in the underground resistance movement.

Jenkin, in particular, was a skilled propagandist. He used his technical expertise to distribute pamphlets and information that exposed the brutality of the apartheid regime. The South African government considered this a serious threat, as it challenged their control over information and inspired others to resist. In 1978, Jenkin and Lee were arrested and charged with distributing ANC literature, a crime that the government treated with utmost seriousness.

At their trial, both men were unapologetic, defending their actions as morally justified in the face of an immoral system. However, their arguments fell on deaf ears, and they were sentenced to lengthy prison terms—Jenkin received 12 years, and Lee was sentenced to 8 years. They were sent to Pretoria Central Prison, a maximum-security facility known for housing political prisoners and notorious for its strict security measures.

Life in Pretoria Central Prison: A Fortress of Despair

Pretoria Central Prison was a forbidding place, designed to break the spirits of those who opposed the apartheid regime. It was heavily fortified, with multiple layers of security that included high walls, electrified fences, armed guards, and a labyrinth of locked doors. The prison was meant to be escape-proof, and its harsh conditions were intended to serve as a deterrent to others who might dare to challenge the government.

For Jenkin, Lee, and other political prisoners, life in Pretoria Central was a daily struggle against despair. They were isolated from the outside world, subjected to constant surveillance, and denied basic freedoms. Despite these conditions, the prisoners found ways to resist, using their confinement as an opportunity to continue the fight against apartheid. They held discussions, shared information, and kept the spirit of resistance alive within the prison walls.

It was during this time that Jenkin began to formulate a plan to escape. He refused to accept the idea of spending years in prison while the fight for freedom continued outside. With his technical skills and a relentless determination, Jenkin started to devise a strategy that would become one of the most ingenious prison escapes in history.

The Escape Plan: An Ingenious Strategy

The escape plan that Tim Jenkin devised was as audacious as it was ingenious. It relied not on brute force or violence, but on careful observation, patience, and an understanding of the prison's inner workings. Jenkin spent months studying the prison's layout, the routines of the guards, and, most importantly, the locks on the doors that held them captive.

Pretoria Central Prison was secured by a series of heavy doors, each with its own lock. To escape, the prisoners would need to unlock each of these doors, moving from the inside of the prison to the outer gates. However, the locks were complex, and the keys were held securely by the guards. Jenkin realized that the only way to escape would be to create his own keys—an idea that seemed almost impossible given the limited resources available in the prison.

Undeterred, Jenkin began to experiment with materials he could find inside the prison. Using smuggled items like wood from a broom handle, he meticulously crafted wooden replicas of the keys he had observed. This process required extreme precision, as even the smallest error would render the keys useless. Over time, Jenkin managed to create a set of wooden keys that could open the various locks in the prison.

Jenkin shared his plan with Stephen Lee and another inmate, Alex Moumbaris, a French national imprisoned for his involvement in the anti-apartheid movement. Together, the three men formed a tight-knit group, united by their desire for freedom. They practiced using the keys, rehearsed their movements, and waited for the right moment to make their move.

The Escape: A Night of Tension and Triumph

The escape took place on the night of December 11, 1979. The three men had carefully chosen the date, knowing that the guards would be more relaxed during the holiday season. They waited until the prison was quiet, then began their daring journey through the labyrinth of locked doors.

Using the wooden keys Jenkin had crafted, the men quietly unlocked door after door, moving deeper into the prison's security system. Each lock they opened brought them closer to freedom, but also increased the risk of being caught. The tension was immense, as even a single mistake could lead to disaster.

The final hurdle was the prison's outer gate, a massive door that stood between them and freedom. With nerves of steel, Jenkin used his wooden key to unlock the gate. As the door swung open, the men stepped outside into the cool night air, free for the first time in months.

They quickly scaled the prison's outer wall and made their way into the streets of Pretoria.

The escape was a success, but the danger was far from over. The men were now fugitives, and the apartheid regime would stop at nothing to capture them. They knew they had to move quickly to avoid detection, and they had prepared for this moment by arranging safe houses and disguises. Over the next few days, they managed to elude the authorities and eventually made their way to Swaziland, a neighboring country that offered sanctuary to anti-apartheid activists.

The Aftermath: A Symbol of Resistance

The escape of Tim Jenkin, Stephen Lee, and Alex Moumbaris from Pretoria Central Prison was a stunning blow to the apartheid regime. It demonstrated that even the most oppressive systems could not crush the human spirit or extinguish the desire for freedom. The story of their escape became a source of inspiration for others in the anti-apartheid movement, showing that resistance was possible even in the face of overwhelming odds.

The South African government, embarrassed by the escape, launched a massive manhunt to recapture the fugitives. However, despite their best efforts, Jenkin and his comrades remained free. They continued their activism from exile, using their experience to draw attention to the injustices of apartheid and rally support for the cause.

For Tim Jenkin, the escape marked the beginning of a new chapter in his life. He became a prominent figure in the anti-apartheid movement, working alongside leaders like Nelson Mandela and Oliver Tambo to dismantle the apartheid system. His story was eventually documented in his autobiography, "Inside Out: Escape from Pretoria Prison," which provided a firsthand account of the daring escape and the broader struggle against apartheid.

Legacy: The Enduring Impact of the Escape

The "Escape from Pretoria" is not just a thrilling story of adventure and ingenuity; it is also a powerful symbol of resistance against tyranny. The courage and determination of Tim Jenkin, Stephen Lee, and Alex Moumbaris continue to inspire those who fight for justice and human rights around the world.

In the years following their escape, South Africa underwent profound changes. The apartheid regime, weakened by internal resistance and international pressure, eventually collapsed. In 1994, Nelson Mandela was elected as South Africa's first black president, ushering in a new era of democracy and reconciliation. The struggle that Jenkin and his comrades had been a part of was finally victorious.

Today, the story of the "Escape from Pretoria" is remembered as one of the many acts of bravery that contributed to the downfall of apartheid. It serves as a reminder that even in the darkest of times, individuals have the power to make a difference. The wooden keys that Tim Jenkin crafted in his prison cell may have been small, but they unlocked not just doors, but the possibility of freedom for an entire nation.

Conclusion

The "Escape from Pretoria" is a story that resonates on multiple levels— as a thrilling tale of ingenuity and daring, as a profound act of political resistance, and as a symbol of the struggle for justice. Tim Jenkin, Stephen Lee, and Alex Moumbaris risked everything for the cause they believed in, and their successful escape from one of South Africa's most secure prisons remains an inspiration to all who stand against oppression. Their story is a testament to the power of the human spirit, the importance of resilience, and the enduring fight for freedom in the face of tyranny.

Chapter 18: Houdini's Jailbreaks

Harry Houdini, born Erik Weisz in 1874, became one of the most famous magicians and escape artists in history. His name is synonymous with daring feats of escapology, and his performances captivated audiences around the world. Among his most famous acts were his jail escapes, where he would challenge police departments to lock him in their most secure cells, only to emerge unscathed and free within minutes. These daring jailbreaks were not just magic tricks; they were demonstrations of Houdini's incredible skill, determination, and ingenuity. The Houdini jailbreaks became legendary, solidifying his reputation as the world's greatest escape artist.

Early Life and the Origins of Escapology

To understand Houdini's remarkable jailbreaks, it is important to explore his early life and how he developed his extraordinary talents. Houdini was born in Budapest, Hungary, but his family moved to the United States when he was just four years old. Growing up in poverty in Wisconsin, Houdini was drawn to the world of magic and performance from a young age. He began performing in small shows and carnivals, initially focusing on card tricks and sleight of hand.

However, Houdini's interest in magic soon expanded to include escapes. He was fascinated by the idea of freeing himself from restraints and began practicing with ropes, handcuffs, and other bindings. His early experiments with escape techniques laid the foundation for what would become his signature performances. Houdini realized that the public was drawn to the suspense and danger of escape acts, and he began to incorporate them into his shows.

Houdini's first major breakthrough came in 1899 when he was discovered by Martin Beck, a vaudeville impresario. Beck recognized

Houdini's potential and encouraged him to focus on escape acts. This advice proved to be pivotal in Houdini's career. He quickly became known as the "Handcuff King," dazzling audiences with his ability to free himself from seemingly impossible situations.

The Beginning of Jail Escapes: A Unique Challenge

Houdini's jail escapes began as a publicity stunt, but they quickly became a hallmark of his performances. The concept was simple yet thrilling: Houdini would visit a city, challenge the local police department to lock him in their most secure cell, and then escape. The police were often skeptical of his abilities and eager to prove that their jails were escape-proof. Houdini, always confident in his skills, accepted the challenge with enthusiasm.

The first of these jail escapes took place in 1899 in Chicago, where Houdini was locked in a cell at the Cook County Jail. The police were confident that Houdini would not be able to escape, as the jail was equipped with state-of-the-art locks and security measures. However, Houdini managed to free himself in a matter of minutes, much to the astonishment of the police and the public. This early success set the stage for many more jailbreaks to come.

Houdini's jail escapes were not just about escaping from the cell; they were also about creating a spectacle. He often allowed the police to strip search him before locking him up, ensuring that he had no hidden tools or keys. He would then enter the cell, seemingly unprepared and defenseless, only to emerge free moments later. The mystery of how he accomplished these escapes added to his allure and made his performances even more captivating.

Techniques and Ingenuity: The Secrets Behind the Escapes

Houdini's jail escapes were a combination of physical skill, mental acuity, and meticulous preparation. While he never fully revealed his methods, several factors contributed to his success.

1. **Lock Picking**: Houdini was an expert locksmith and spent years honing his ability to pick locks. He studied the mechanisms of different locks and developed techniques to manipulate them quickly and efficiently. He often carried concealed lock-picking tools, which he could use to open handcuffs, cell doors, and other restraints.

2. **Concealed Tools**: Despite being searched before his performances, Houdini was adept at hiding small tools on his person. He might conceal a key in his mouth, under his tongue, or even in a secret pocket sewn into his clothing. In some cases, he used flexible wires or other devices that could be hidden in his hair or under his skin.

3. **Flexibility and Physical Conditioning**: Houdini's physical abilities were also crucial to his success. He was incredibly flexible, which allowed him to contort his body to escape from tight spaces or slip out of restraints. He also trained his body to endure pain and discomfort, enabling him to perform dangerous stunts with minimal risk.

4. **Mental Preparation**: Houdini's escapes required immense mental focus and determination. He had to remain calm under pressure, even when faced with seemingly insurmountable obstacles. His ability to stay composed and think clearly in high-stress situations was a key factor in his success.

5. **Misdirection and Psychological Manipulation**: Houdini was a master of misdirection. He often used psychological tactics to distract or confuse his captors, making them believe he was struggling or failing when, in reality, he was on the

verge of escape. His ability to manipulate the perceptions of his audience and captors added an extra layer of intrigue to his performances.

Famous Jailbreaks: Escaping from the World's Most Secure Prisons

Throughout his career, Houdini performed dozens of jail escapes, each one more daring and elaborate than the last. Some of his most famous jailbreaks include:

1. **The Washington, D.C. Jail Escape (1906)**: In 1906, Houdini was challenged to escape from the United States Jail in Washington, D.C. The jail was known for its high security, and the warden was confident that Houdini would not be able to escape. Houdini was stripped naked, searched thoroughly, and locked in a cell. Within minutes, he had freed himself and was standing outside the jail, much to the astonishment of the warden and the gathered crowd.

2. **The Boston Tombs (1906)**: The Boston Tombs was a notorious prison in Massachusetts, known for its impenetrable cells and strict security measures. Houdini accepted a challenge to escape from this prison, which had held some of the most dangerous criminals in the state. Once again, Houdini was stripped and locked in a cell. To the amazement of the authorities, he escaped in just a few minutes, leaving the cell door wide open as proof of his feat.

3. **The Moscow Jail Escape (1903)**: In 1903, Houdini traveled to Russia, where he was challenged to escape from a prison in Moscow. The Russian authorities were eager to prove that their jails were escape-proof, and they took extra precautions to ensure that Houdini would not be able to escape. Despite these efforts, Houdini managed to free himself in a matter of minutes, stunning the Russian officials and solidifying his

reputation as the world's greatest escape artist.

4. **The British Prisons**: Houdini also performed several jailbreaks in the United Kingdom, including escapes from some of the country's most secure prisons. One of his most famous escapes took place in Manchester, where he was locked in a cell at the city's central police station. Houdini escaped with ease, much to the disbelief of the British authorities. His performances in the UK further cemented his international fame.

5. **The Hamburg Jail Escape (1902)**: During a tour of Europe, Houdini accepted a challenge to escape from a jail in Hamburg, Germany. The jail was considered one of the most secure in the country, and the authorities were confident that Houdini would not be able to escape. However, Houdini's reputation preceded him, and a large crowd gathered to witness the event. In typical fashion, Houdini escaped in a matter of minutes, leaving the German authorities baffled.

6. **The Montreal Jail Escape (1915)**: Houdini's jailbreaks were not limited to the United States and Europe. During his tour in Canada, Houdini was challenged to escape from the Montreal jail, which was known for its heavy iron doors and sophisticated locking mechanisms. Despite the local authorities' confidence, Houdini managed to free himself in a matter of minutes, further reinforcing his status as the "Handcuff King."

Publicity and the Cult of Personality

Houdini's jail escapes were not just feats of physical and mental prowess; they were also carefully crafted publicity stunts. Houdini understood the power of the media and used it to his advantage. Each escape was widely publicized, with newspapers covering his challenges and performances in detail. Houdini often invited reporters to witness his escapes firsthand, ensuring that his feats were documented and shared with a wide audience.

Houdini's larger-than-life personality also contributed to his success. He cultivated an image of invincibility, presenting himself as a fearless and unstoppable force. His escapes were framed as battles of wits between himself and the authorities, with Houdini always emerging victorious. This narrative resonated with the public, who saw Houdini as a symbol of defiance and freedom.

Houdini's ability to generate publicity was not limited to his jail escapes. He also performed other daring stunts, such as escaping from locked safes, submerged crates, and straightjackets suspended high above the ground. Each performance was designed to capture the public's imagination and reinforce Houdini's reputation as the world's greatest escape artist.

The Skeptics and the Legacy of Houdini's Escapes

Despite his fame, Houdini faced skepticism from some quarters. Critics claimed that his escapes were rigged or that he had inside help from sympathetic jailers. Houdini always denied these accusations, insisting that his escapes were the result of his skill and preparation. To prove his detractors wrong, Houdini often invited independent observers to verify the conditions of his escapes, ensuring that there was no possibility of cheating.

Houdini's jail escapes had a lasting impact on the world of magic and entertainment. His performances inspired a new generation of magicians and escape artists, many of whom sought to emulate his daring feats. Houdini's influence can be seen in the work of later performers like David Copperfield, David Blaine, and Criss Angel, who have continued to push the boundaries of what is possible in magic and escapology.

Beyond his impact on the world of magic, Houdini's jail escapes also left a cultural legacy. His name became synonymous with escape and freedom, and his story continues to be told in books, films, and documentaries. Houdini's life and career have become the stuff of legend, and his escapes remain some of the most iconic moments in the history of entertainment.

Conclusion

Harry Houdini's jailbreaks were not just incredible feats of escapology; they were also powerful statements of ingenuity, skill, and determination. Through his daring escapes from some of the world's most secure jails, Houdini captivated audiences and solidified his reputation as the greatest escape artist of all time. His ability to free himself from seemingly impossible situations, combined with his flair for showmanship and publicity, made him a global sensation.

Houdini's jailbreaks continue to inspire and fascinate people to this day. His legacy as a master escape artist lives on, not only in the world of magic but also in the broader cultural imagination. Houdini's story is a testament to the power of human creativity and resilience, and his jailbreaks remain some of the most remarkable and enduring achievements in the history of performance.

Chapter 19: Escape from Wormwood Scrubs

Wormwood Scrubs, a high-security prison in West London, has long been one of the most infamous institutions in the British penal system. Built in the late 19th century, it has housed some of the most dangerous criminals in the UK. Despite its reputation as a formidable fortress, Wormwood Scrubs has been the site of numerous escape attempts over the years. However, one of the most remarkable incidents in the prison's history is the daring escape of two IRA prisoners in 1991, a meticulously planned and executed operation that captured national attention and left an indelible mark on the history of British prisons.

The History of Wormwood Scrubs

Wormwood Scrubs Prison, commonly known simply as "The Scrubs," was opened in 1874. It was initially designed to hold prisoners awaiting trial, as well as those serving short sentences. Over the years, it evolved into a high-security facility, housing some of the most notorious criminals in the UK, including gangsters, terrorists, and high-profile offenders.

The prison's design, like many Victorian-era institutions, was meant to embody the principles of order and control. The main prison building, constructed of yellow brick, was surrounded by high walls topped with razor wire, and the complex was guarded by watchtowers and heavily armed officers. Inside, the layout was intended to enforce discipline, with long, narrow corridors and small cells. The architecture reflected the harsh penal philosophies of the time, emphasizing punishment over rehabilitation.

Despite its imposing structure, Wormwood Scrubs has seen numerous escape attempts over the years. These escapes have ranged from the simple and spontaneous to the highly organized and daring. The 1991 escape of two IRA prisoners, however, stands out as one of the most audacious and well-planned in the prison's history.

The Political Context: The IRA and British Prisons

To understand the significance of the escape from Wormwood Scrubs, it is essential to consider the political context of the time. The Irish Republican Army (IRA) was engaged in a violent campaign against British rule in Northern Ireland, a conflict that had persisted for decades. The IRA's activities included bombings, assassinations, and other acts of terrorism, both in Northern Ireland and on the British mainland. As a result, many IRA members were imprisoned in the UK, and British prisons became key battlegrounds in the conflict.

IRA prisoners were often seen as political prisoners by their supporters, and many refused to accept the authority of the British state. This led to numerous protests, hunger strikes, and escape attempts by IRA inmates. The British government, for its part, was determined to maintain control over these prisoners and prevent them from becoming symbols of resistance. Wormwood Scrubs, with its high-security status, was seen as a crucial part of this effort.

By the early 1990s, the situation had reached a boiling point. The IRA was still active, and tensions between the British government and Irish republican groups remained high. In this climate, the escape from Wormwood Scrubs took on a significance far beyond a simple prison break—it became a symbolic act of defiance against the British state.

The Escape Plan: A Masterpiece of Cunning and Deception

The escape from Wormwood Scrubs in 1991 involved two IRA prisoners: Pearse McAuley and Nessan Quinlivan. Both men were highly committed members of the IRA and had been convicted of serious offenses related to their activities. McAuley and Quinlivan, like many IRA prisoners, refused to accept the legitimacy of their imprisonment and were determined to escape.

The plan for the escape was both daring and meticulously organized. It involved not only the prisoners themselves but also external accomplices who played crucial roles in the operation. The escape took advantage of a combination of factors, including weaknesses in the prison's security systems, the element of surprise, and the careful planning of every detail.

One of the key elements of the escape was the use of deception. The prisoners managed to obtain information about the prison's routines and security measures, which allowed them to exploit weaknesses in the system. For example, they learned about the timing of guard shifts and the layout of the prison, which helped them plan the timing of their escape.

On the day of the escape, McAuley and Quinlivan were being escorted to a visit with their solicitor. This was a routine procedure, but the prisoners had managed to obtain firearms that had been smuggled into the prison by their accomplices. As they were being escorted through the prison, they drew their weapons and took the guards by surprise. The guards were overpowered, and the prisoners made their way to the prison's outer perimeter.

Outside the prison, a getaway car was waiting, driven by one of the IRA's external operatives. The prisoners quickly got into the car, and the vehicle sped away from Wormwood Scrubs, leaving the prison's guards and security systems powerless to stop them. The entire operation was executed with such precision that by the time the alarm was raised, McAuley and Quinlivan were already far from the prison.

The Aftermath: A National Manhunt and Political Fallout

The escape from Wormwood Scrubs sent shockwaves through the British government and the public. The idea that two high-profile IRA prisoners could escape from one of the country's most secure prisons was seen as a major embarrassment for the authorities. A massive manhunt was launched to recapture the fugitives, involving the police, military, and intelligence services.

The media quickly picked up on the story, and the escape became front-page news across the UK. The public was both shocked and fascinated by the audacity of the escape, and the story took on a life of its own. For the IRA, the escape was a propaganda coup, reinforcing the image of their members as fearless and resourceful fighters against British rule.

The British government, however, was deeply concerned about the implications of the escape. The incident raised serious questions about the security of British prisons, particularly in relation to high-risk political prisoners. The government faced criticism from both the public and opposition parties, who accused it of failing to adequately protect national security.

In response to the escape, the British authorities launched a series of inquiries and reviews into prison security. New measures were introduced to prevent similar incidents in the future, including increased surveillance, tighter controls on visits, and enhanced vetting of prison staff. The escape also led to a reevaluation of the handling of IRA prisoners, with some arguing that they should be treated differently from ordinary criminals due to the political nature of their offenses.

Despite the extensive manhunt, McAuley and Quinlivan managed to evade capture for some time. They eventually fled the UK and made their way to the Republic of Ireland, where they continued to be active in the republican movement. Their escape became a symbol of resistance and defiance for many within the IRA and its supporters.

The Legacy of the Escape: Lessons Learned and Unanswered Questions

The escape from Wormwood Scrubs in 1991 left a lasting impact on the British prison system and the public's perception of security. The incident highlighted the vulnerabilities in even the most secure institutions and demonstrated the lengths to which determined prisoners could go to regain their freedom.

One of the key lessons from the escape was the importance of intelligence and information security. The fact that the prisoners had managed to obtain detailed information about the prison's routines and security measures was a major factor in their success. This led to increased efforts to protect sensitive information within prisons and to prevent inmates from gaining access to such details.

Another lesson was the need for constant vigilance and adaptability in prison security. The escape showed that even routine procedures, such as prisoner escorts, could be exploited if security personnel became complacent. As a result, prisons across the UK implemented stricter protocols for handling high-risk prisoners, including more rigorous searches, increased supervision, and the use of specialized security teams.

The escape also raised broader questions about the role of prisons in dealing with political prisoners and the potential for such prisoners to use their incarceration as a platform for protest and resistance. The British government continued to grapple with these issues throughout the 1990s, particularly in relation to the ongoing conflict in Northern Ireland.

In popular culture, the escape from Wormwood Scrubs has become one of the most famous prison break stories in British history. It has been the subject of numerous books, documentaries, and articles, each examining the details of the escape and its wider implications. The story of McAuley and Quinlivan's escape continues to capture the imagination, both as a tale of daring and as a reflection of the complex political landscape of the time.

Conclusion

The escape from Wormwood Scrubs in 1991 stands as one of the most audacious and well-planned prison breaks in British history. It was an event that not only embarrassed the British government and exposed vulnerabilities in the prison system but also served as a powerful symbol of resistance for the IRA and its supporters.

The meticulous planning and execution of the escape, combined with the broader political context in which it occurred, make it a fascinating case study in both criminal ingenuity and the challenges of maintaining security in high-risk environments. The legacy of the escape continues to be felt in the UK, both in the ongoing efforts to improve prison security and in the enduring fascination with stories of daring and defiance.

As with many such events, the escape from Wormwood Scrubs is a reminder that even the most secure institutions are not infallible and that the determination of individuals to reclaim their freedom can sometimes overcome even the most formidable obstacles. The story of McAuley and Quinlivan's escape remains a testament to the enduring power of human ingenuity and the lengths to which people will go to achieve their goals.

Chapter 20: Escape from Maze Prison

The escape from Maze Prison in Northern Ireland is one of the most significant and audacious prison breaks in modern history. Taking place on September 25, 1983, it involved the successful escape of 38 prisoners, all of whom were members of the Provisional Irish Republican Army (IRA), a paramilitary organization engaged in a violent campaign against British rule in Northern Ireland. This event, known as the "Great Escape," was not just a prison break; it was a meticulously planned operation that highlighted the political tensions of the time and had far-reaching consequences for the conflict known as "The Troubles."

The Maze Prison: A Symbol of the Northern Ireland Conflict

Maze Prison, also known as Long Kesh, was located near Lisburn, about 10 miles from Belfast. It was established in 1971 and quickly became one of the most notorious prisons in the United Kingdom. During the Troubles, the conflict between nationalist/republican and unionist/loyalist communities in Northern Ireland, the prison held many political prisoners, including members of the IRA and loyalist paramilitary groups.

The Maze was a high-security prison, designed to house the most dangerous and politically motivated prisoners. It was divided into "H-blocks," so named because of their shape, and each block housed several cells. The prison's reputation was cemented by the hunger strikes of 1981, in which IRA prisoners protested for political status, leading to the death of ten prisoners, including the famous Bobby Sands. The prison was thus a central battleground in the struggle between the British government and Irish republicans.

For the IRA, escaping from the Maze was not just about freedom; it was a political act, a symbolic victory against the British state. The escape that took place in 1983 was the culmination of months of planning and preparation by the prisoners and their supporters outside the prison.

Planning the Escape: A Complex Operation

The escape from Maze Prison was not a spontaneous act; it was a highly organized operation that involved careful planning, deception, and coordination between the prisoners and their external network. The IRA prisoners at the Maze were among the most committed and disciplined members of the organization, and they approached the escape as a military operation.

One of the key elements of the escape plan was the smuggling of weapons into the prison. Over several months, the prisoners managed to acquire six handguns, which were hidden within the prison. These weapons would later be used to overpower the guards during the escape. The smuggling operation was facilitated by the prisoners' outside contacts, who were able to exploit weaknesses in the prison's security procedures.

Another crucial aspect of the plan was the prisoners' ability to gather intelligence about the prison's routines and security measures. The IRA inmates used their time in the prison workshops and other areas to observe the movements of guards and identify potential vulnerabilities. They also managed to acquire uniforms and other items that would help them blend in with prison staff during the escape.

The planning also involved creating a diversion to distract the guards and cover the escapees' movements. This was achieved through a combination of fake illnesses, work slowdowns, and other disruptions that kept the prison staff occupied while the escape was being carried out.

The Escape: A Bold and Coordinated Effort

The escape from Maze Prison took place on the afternoon of September 25, 1983. It was a Sunday, a day when the prison was usually quieter, with fewer staff on duty. The escape began when a group of IRA prisoners took control of H-Block 7, where they were housed. They used the smuggled handguns to overpower the prison guards, taking several of them hostage. The prisoners then disguised themselves as guards and used their uniforms to move through the prison without raising suspicion.

The prisoners' plan relied on timing and coordination. As they moved through the prison, they disabled the alarm systems and communication lines to prevent the guards from raising the alarm. They also took control of the prison's control room, which allowed them to open the gates and facilitate their escape.

The escape was not without violence. During the operation, several guards were injured, and one guard, James Ferris, tragically lost his life after being stabbed. The prisoners' use of force was a reflection of the high stakes involved and their determination to succeed.

Once outside the prison, the escapees made their way to a series of waiting vehicles, which had been arranged by the IRA's external network. The vehicles were used to transport the escapees to safe houses, where they could hide and evade capture. The escapees had planned their routes carefully, and many of them were able to reach their destinations without being detected by the authorities.

The Aftermath: A Massive Manhunt and Political Fallout

The escape from Maze Prison was a major embarrassment for the British government and the prison authorities. The fact that 38 high-profile IRA prisoners had managed to escape from what was supposed to be one of the most secure prisons in the UK raised serious questions about the effectiveness of the prison's security measures.

In the immediate aftermath of the escape, a massive manhunt was launched to recapture the fugitives. Thousands of police officers, soldiers, and intelligence agents were deployed across Northern Ireland and the Republic of Ireland to track down the escapees. Roadblocks were set up, and helicopters were used to search the countryside. Despite these efforts, many of the escapees managed to evade capture for days, weeks, and even months.

Within the first few days, some of the escapees were recaptured, but others managed to cross the border into the Republic of Ireland, where they were beyond the reach of British law enforcement. A few of the escapees even made it to the United States and other countries, where they sought refuge.

The political fallout from the escape was significant. The British government faced intense criticism from both the public and the opposition parties, who accused it of failing to protect national security. The escape also fueled tensions between the British government and the Irish republican movement, which saw the escape as a victory against British oppression.

The escape from Maze Prison also had a psychological impact on both sides of the conflict. For the IRA and its supporters, the escape was a major morale boost, demonstrating that the organization could strike a blow against the British state even from within the walls of a maximum-security prison. For the British government and the security forces, the escape was a stark reminder of the challenges they faced in containing the IRA and maintaining order in Northern Ireland.

The Legacy of the Escape: Changes in Prison Security and the Peace Process

The escape from Maze Prison in 1983 led to significant changes in the way prisons in Northern Ireland and the rest of the UK were managed. In the aftermath of the escape, the British government conducted a thorough review of prison security and implemented a range of measures to prevent similar incidents in the future.

One of the key changes was the introduction of more stringent security protocols, including increased surveillance, tighter control over prison staff, and more rigorous checks on visitors. The prison authorities also invested in new technology, such as electronic locks and security cameras, to improve their ability to monitor and control the prison environment.

The escape also had an impact on the broader political situation in Northern Ireland. In the years following the escape, the British government and the Irish republican movement engaged in a series of negotiations that ultimately led to the signing of the Good Friday Agreement in 1998. The agreement, which brought an end to the conflict in Northern Ireland, included provisions for the release of political prisoners, including many of those who had been involved in the escape from Maze Prison.

For the IRA and its supporters, the escape from Maze Prison remains a symbol of resistance and defiance against British rule. The escape is often celebrated in republican communities, and the stories of the escapees have become part of the folklore of the conflict.

Conclusion

The escape from Maze Prison in 1983 stands as one of the most remarkable and daring prison breaks in modern history. It was an event that not only highlighted the deep political divisions in Northern

Ireland but also demonstrated the lengths to which the IRA and its members were willing to go in their struggle against British rule.

The meticulous planning and execution of the escape, combined with the broader political context in which it took place, make it a fascinating case study in both criminal ingenuity and the challenges of maintaining security in high-risk environments. The escape from Maze Prison remains a powerful reminder of the complex and often tragic history of Northern Ireland and the enduring impact of the Troubles on the people of the region.

Chapter 21: Escape from Tower of London

The Tower of London, with its imposing stone walls and storied history, stands as one of the most famous landmarks in the world. For nearly a thousand years, it has served as a royal palace, a fortress, and, most notoriously, a prison. The Tower has housed some of the most high-profile prisoners in English history, from disgraced nobles to political dissidents and even members of the royal family. For many, imprisonment in the Tower of London was synonymous with a death sentence, with few ever leaving its grim confines alive.

Yet, amid the tales of executions and political intrigue, there are also stories of incredible escapes. Though the Tower was designed to be impenetrable, a few daring souls managed to defy the odds and break free from its grasp. The escapes from the Tower of London are not just remarkable feats of courage and ingenuity; they are also windows into the tumultuous history of England, reflecting the power struggles and conflicts that have shaped the nation.

The Tower of London: A Fortress and Prison

Before delving into the dramatic escapes from the Tower, it is essential to understand the significance of the structure itself. The Tower of London was founded in 1066 as part of the Norman Conquest of England. Over the centuries, it was expanded and fortified, becoming one of the most formidable castles in Europe. The White Tower, the oldest part of the complex, was constructed by William the Conqueror as a symbol of Norman power.

While the Tower served many roles, its use as a prison is perhaps its most infamous. From the 12th century onward, it became a place of incarceration for those who posed a threat to the crown, whether they were political adversaries, rebellious nobles, or even royalty. The Tower's reputation for holding—and often executing—those who crossed the monarchy earned it a fearsome reputation.

Given the Tower's design and purpose, escaping from its confines seemed nearly impossible. The prison was heavily guarded, and the surrounding waters of the River Thames provided an additional natural barrier. Yet, despite these challenges, there were several successful escapes, each with its own story of cunning, courage, and luck.

The Escape of Ranulf Flambard (1101): The First Great Escape

One of the earliest and most famous escapes from the Tower of London took place in 1101 and involved Ranulf Flambard, the Bishop of Durham. Flambard was a powerful figure in the court of King William II, known as William Rufus. He was the king's chief financial officer and was responsible for raising taxes, a task that earned him many enemies. After William Rufus's death, his successor, Henry I, accused Flambard of embezzlement and had him imprisoned in the Tower.

Flambard's escape is notable not only because it was the first recorded escape from the Tower but also because of the cleverness with which it was carried out. Flambard, a shrewd and resourceful man, used his charm to befriend his guards. He also arranged for a group of loyal supporters to smuggle a rope into the Tower, hidden inside a barrel of wine. On February 2, 1101, during a feast in his cell, Flambard distracted his captors with food and drink. When the guards were sufficiently inebriated, Flambard used the rope to lower himself from a high window of the White Tower. He then made his way to the River Thames, where a boat was waiting to whisk him to safety.

Flambard's escape was a humiliating blow to King Henry I, who had hoped to make an example of his former minister. Instead, Flambard fled to Normandy, where he joined forces with Henry's brother, Robert

Curthose, in an attempt to reclaim the English throne. Though the rebellion ultimately failed, Flambard's escape remains one of the most legendary in the Tower's history.

John Gerard (1597): A Jesuit's Great Escape

The story of John Gerard's escape from the Tower of London is one of the most dramatic and daring in the annals of the prison. Gerard, a Jesuit priest, was imprisoned in the Tower during the reign of Queen Elizabeth I as part of the government's efforts to suppress Catholicism. His escape, which took place in 1597, is often regarded as one of the most audacious in history.

Gerard was arrested in 1594 and subjected to torture in an effort to extract information about other Catholics and priests. Despite the brutal treatment, Gerard refused to betray his fellow believers. He was eventually confined to a cell in the Tower, awaiting further interrogation or execution. It was during this time that Gerard began to plan his escape.

Gerard's escape plan hinged on the cooperation of allies both inside and outside the Tower. He managed to communicate with fellow Catholics through secret messages smuggled in and out of the prison. With the help of these contacts, Gerard arranged for a rope to be delivered to him in his cell.

On the night of October 3, 1597, Gerard put his plan into action. With the help of a fellow prisoner, John Arden, Gerard climbed out of his cell window and used the rope to lower himself down the outer wall of the Tower. The descent was perilous, as the walls of the Tower were sheer and treacherous, but Gerard's determination saw him through.

Once he reached the ground, Gerard made his way to the River Thames, where a boat, arranged by his contacts, was waiting to take him to safety. The escape was a remarkable success, and Gerard was able to flee to the continent, where he continued his work as a Jesuit priest.

Gerard later wrote a detailed account of his escape, which became a source of inspiration for Catholics and other persecuted groups. His story is a testament to the power of faith, courage, and the human spirit's determination to resist oppression.

The Escape of the Duke of Orleans (1356): A Royal Prisoner's Daring Escape

Another remarkable escape from the Tower of London involved Charles, Duke of Orleans, a French nobleman who was captured by the English during the Hundred Years' War. Charles was taken prisoner following the Battle of Agincourt in 1415 and was held in the Tower for several years.

Charles's captivity in the Tower was relatively comfortable compared to the conditions faced by many other prisoners. As a high-ranking noble, he was treated with a degree of respect and was allowed certain privileges, including the ability to correspond with his family and friends in France. However, his status as a prisoner of war meant that he was still under constant guard, and the possibility of escape seemed remote.

Despite these challenges, Charles was determined to regain his freedom. His escape plan involved bribing several of the Tower's guards, who agreed to turn a blind eye to his activities. On the night of his escape, Charles disguised himself as a servant and slipped past the guards. He then made his way to the Tower's outer walls, where a rope had been lowered by his accomplices on the outside.

Charles's escape was a bold and daring act, made all the more remarkable by the fact that he was able to evade capture and make his way back to France. Once free, Charles resumed his role as a prominent figure in French politics and continued to play a significant role in the ongoing conflict between England and France.

The Escape of Lady Arabella Stuart (1611): A Royal Tragedy

Lady Arabella Stuart's attempted escape from the Tower of London in 1611 is a tragic tale of love, power, and desperation. Arabella was a member of the royal family, a cousin of King James I, and a potential heir to the throne. Her royal blood made her a pawn in the power struggles of the time, and her secret marriage to William Seymour, another potential claimant to the throne, alarmed the king. As a result, both Arabella and Seymour were imprisoned—Arabella in the Tower of London and Seymour in the Tower of Lambeth.

Desperate to be reunited with her husband and fearing for her life, Arabella hatched a plan to escape from the Tower. On June 3, 1611, she disguised herself as a man and managed to slip past the guards. Meanwhile, Seymour also escaped from his confinement, and the two planned to meet and flee the country together.

However, the couple's luck ran out. While Seymour managed to reach the safety of the continent, Arabella's escape was thwarted. She was recaptured and returned to the Tower, where she spent the rest of her life in captivity. Arabella's story is a poignant reminder of the dangers faced by those who dared to defy the crown, and her tragic fate continues to resonate with those who study the history of the Tower of London.

The Escape of Edmund Campion (1581): A Martyr's Narrow Escape

Edmund Campion, a Jesuit priest and missionary, was another notable figure who attempted to escape from the Tower of London during the reign of Elizabeth I. Campion was arrested in 1581 as part of the government's crackdown on Catholic priests, and he was subjected to intense interrogation and torture in an effort to force him to renounce his faith.

Despite the harsh conditions of his imprisonment, Campion remained steadfast in his beliefs. His escape attempt came as part of a broader effort by Catholic sympathizers to free imprisoned priests and other religious dissidents. Campion's supporters arranged for a disguise and a safe route out of the Tower, but the plan was ultimately foiled, and Campion was recaptured.

Campion's escape attempt ended in tragedy, as he was executed for his faith later that year. However, his story remains a powerful testament to the resilience and determination of those who fought for religious freedom during a time of intense persecution.

Conclusion: The Legacy of Escapes from the Tower of London

The escapes from the Tower of London are more than just thrilling tales of adventure and daring; they are reflections of the broader historical forces that shaped England and the world. Each escape, successful or not, tells a story of resistance, defiance, and the indomitable human spirit.

For centuries, the Tower of London has stood as a symbol of royal power and authority, but the escapes from its confines remind us that even the most formidable walls can be breached. Whether through cunning, bravery, or sheer determination, the prisoners who managed to escape from the Tower of London left a lasting legacy that continues to captivate and inspire.

The stories of these escapes also serve as reminders of the complex and often brutal nature of power, politics, and justice in history. From political prisoners to religious dissidents, the individuals who escaped from the Tower of London were often caught up in the struggles of their time, and their stories offer valuable insights into the challenges and conflicts that shaped their world.

Today, the Tower of London stands as a historical monument, attracting millions of visitors from around the world. While it is no longer a functioning prison, its history as a place of incarceration, execution, and escape continues to resonate. The stories of those who escaped from the Tower are a testament to the enduring human desire for freedom and the lengths to which people will go to achieve it.

Chapter 22: Escape from Attica Prison

The term "Attica Prison" instantly evokes images of one of the most infamous uprisings in American history, the Attica Prison Riot of 1971. However, before and after the tragic events of that year, Attica Correctional Facility in New York State was known as a maximum-security prison with an unforgiving reputation. Within its walls, countless inmates have dreamt of escaping its iron grip, but few have managed to do so. Those who succeeded in breaking out of Attica confronted not only the physical barriers of the prison but also the psychological toll of incarceration in one of the most feared institutions in the United States.

The escapes from Attica Prison are as varied as they are dramatic. Over the years, multiple attempts have been made, with a few individuals succeeding in slipping through the cracks of the heavily fortified facility. Each escape tells a unique story of courage, desperation, and the will to defy an environment that sought to crush the spirit of those within its walls.

Attica Correctional Facility: A Fortress of Confinement

Attica Correctional Facility, located in rural western New York State, was constructed in 1930 and was designed to hold the most dangerous and disruptive inmates in the state's prison system. With its high stone walls, guard towers, and heavily fortified gates, Attica was considered virtually escape-proof. The prison's layout was intended to control and monitor every movement within its walls, from the cell blocks to the yard, to the mess hall.

The prison quickly gained a reputation for its harsh conditions. Inmates were subjected to strict discipline, often under the threat of violence from guards. The cold, impersonal architecture of the prison reflected the broader attitude of the time toward incarceration, which emphasized punishment over rehabilitation.

Despite its fearsome reputation, Attica has seen several daring escape attempts throughout its history. These escapes reveal much about the ingenuity of those incarcerated there, as well as the oppressive conditions that drove them to risk everything for a chance at freedom.

Early Escape Attempts: Setting the Stage

Before the infamous riot of 1971, Attica Correctional Facility had already seen its share of escape attempts. In the early decades of the prison's operation, inmates tested the limits of the facility's security, using whatever means they could muster to try to break free.

One of the first significant escape attempts occurred in 1941 when a group of prisoners managed to overpower a guard and scale one of the prison's outer walls. However, the attempt was quickly thwarted, and the prisoners were recaptured before they could get far. This incident underscored the difficulty of escaping from a facility as well-guarded as Attica. Yet, it also demonstrated that even in such a seemingly impregnable fortress, the desire for freedom could not be entirely suppressed.

Over the years, other inmates tried their luck, often with similarly unsuccessful results. These early escape attempts were typically crude and poorly planned, reflecting the desperate circumstances of the prisoners involved. However, each failed attempt provided valuable lessons for future escapees, who would go on to refine their methods and strategies.

The 1971 Uprising: A Turning Point

No discussion of Attica Prison would be complete without addressing the 1971 uprising, an event that fundamentally changed the institution and the broader American penal system. On September 9, 1971, nearly 1,300 inmates took control of the prison, seizing hostages and demanding better living conditions, fair treatment, and political rights. The uprising was fueled by years of mistreatment, overcrowding, and racial tensions within the prison.

For four days, the prisoners held the facility, negotiating with state officials for improved conditions. However, the negotiations ultimately broke down, and on September 13, New York State Governor Nelson Rockefeller ordered a massive assault on the prison to retake control. The assault resulted in the deaths of 43 people, including 10 hostages and 33 inmates. The brutal suppression of the uprising shocked the nation and exposed the deep flaws in the American prison system.

While the uprising itself was not an escape attempt, it highlighted the extreme conditions that drove inmates to desperate measures. The events of 1971 cast a long shadow over Attica, shaping the prison's reputation and influencing the nature of future escape attempts. The riot also led to significant changes in the way the prison was managed, with authorities tightening security and imposing even harsher conditions on the inmates.

The 1976 Escape: A Daring Bid for Freedom

One of the most dramatic and successful escapes from Attica took place in 1976. This escape involved three inmates who managed to break out of the prison using a combination of cunning and meticulous planning. The escapees—Richard Matt, David Sweat, and another inmate—took advantage of a work detail to stage their breakout.

The inmates had been assigned to work in the prison's maintenance shop, which provided them with access to tools and materials that were not available to the general inmate population. Over several months, they carefully crafted a plan to escape. They used their work assignments as cover to dig a tunnel from the shop to the outside of the prison walls.

The escape required an extraordinary level of patience and determination. The inmates had to chip away at the concrete walls and floors of the prison without drawing the attention of the guards. They also had to smuggle the debris out of the work area, a task that required ingenuity and resourcefulness.

On the night of the escape, the inmates made their way through the tunnel they had dug, emerging outside the prison walls. They had to navigate through several layers of security, including fences and guard towers, but they managed to avoid detection. Once outside the prison, they fled into the surrounding countryside, hoping to evade capture.

The escape set off a massive manhunt, with law enforcement agencies from across the state mobilized to track down the fugitives. Despite the intensive search efforts, the escapees managed to elude capture for several days. Their escape became a major news story, capturing the public's imagination and drawing attention to the conditions within Attica.

Ultimately, the escapees were recaptured, but their daring breakout remains one of the most remarkable episodes in the prison's history. The escape also exposed vulnerabilities in Attica's security and led to further changes in the way the prison was managed.

The 2003 Escape Attempt: The Tunnel Plan

In 2003, Attica was the site of another high-profile escape attempt, this time involving a group of inmates who had hatched an elaborate plan to tunnel their way out of the prison. The inmates, who were part of a work crew assigned to the prison's maintenance department, had access to tools and equipment that allowed them to dig a tunnel beneath the prison walls.

The plan was both ambitious and audacious. The inmates spent months digging the tunnel, carefully concealing their activities from the guards. They even constructed a ventilation system to prevent the tunnel from collapsing and to ensure that they could breathe while working underground.

However, the escape attempt was ultimately foiled when prison officials discovered the tunnel just days before the inmates planned to make their move. The discovery was the result of a routine inspection, during which guards noticed signs of unusual activity in the maintenance area.

The foiled escape attempt led to a crackdown on security within the prison, with authorities imposing stricter controls on inmate work assignments and increasing surveillance. The incident also highlighted the lengths to which inmates were willing to go to escape from the harsh conditions of Attica.

The 2015 Escape of Richard Matt and David Sweat: A Modern-Day Prison Break

One of the most famous modern escapes from a New York prison involved two inmates who had previously been housed in Attica: Richard Matt and David Sweat. While their 2015 escape took place from the Clinton Correctional Facility, their earlier incarceration at Attica and the similarities between the two prisons make it a relevant part of the story of escapes from Attica.

Matt and Sweat's escape was a meticulously planned operation that involved the help of a civilian prison employee, Joyce Mitchell, who provided them with tools and other materials needed for their breakout. The inmates spent months sawing through the walls of their cells, using the tools provided by Mitchell to cut through metal and concrete.

Their escape was reminiscent of classic prison break stories, involving crawling through tunnels, navigating steam pipes, and emerging outside the prison walls. Once free, the pair embarked on a weeks-long flight from law enforcement, leading to one of the largest manhunts in New York State history.

Although the escape did not occur at Attica, Matt and Sweat's earlier time at the facility highlighted the challenges of incarcerating determined and resourceful inmates in high-security prisons. The incident also drew attention to the broader issues of prison security and the relationships between inmates and staff.

Lessons from Attica: Security, Reform, and the Future

The history of escapes from Attica Correctional Facility offers valuable lessons about the nature of imprisonment, security, and the human desire for freedom. Despite the prison's reputation as a fortress, inmates have repeatedly found ways to challenge the system and make daring bids for freedom.

These escapes underscore the ingenuity and determination of the incarcerated, as well as the limitations of even the most secure institutions. They also highlight the ongoing need for prison reform and the importance of addressing the underlying issues that lead to such desperate acts.

The escapes from Attica have also had a lasting impact on the broader criminal justice system. They have led to changes in prison management, security protocols, and the treatment of inmates. In the wake of each escape, authorities have been forced to confront the realities of life inside the prison and the need for a more humane approach to incarceration.

Conclusion: The Enduring Legacy of Escape

The story of escapes from Attica Prison is a testament to the enduring human spirit and the lengths to which people will go to seek freedom. From the early escape attempts of the 1940s to the dramatic breakouts of the 21st century, these stories offer a window into the challenges and struggles faced by those behind bars.

While Attica remains one of the most secure prisons in the United States, the history of escapes from the facility serves as a reminder that no prison is entirely escape-proof. The desire for freedom is a powerful force, one that can drive individuals to take extraordinary risks and overcome seemingly insurmountable obstacles.

As Attica continues to evolve and change in response to the challenges of the modern era, the stories of those who have escaped from its walls will continue to resonate. These tales of courage, ingenuity, and determination will remain an important part of the prison's legacy and a reminder of the complex and often fraught relationship between justice, security, and the human need for liberty.

Chapter 23: Escape from San Quentin

San Quentin State Prison, located in California, is one of the most notorious and oldest correctional facilities in the United States. Established in 1852, it has housed some of the most dangerous criminals in American history. Over the years, numerous escape attempts have been made from this formidable institution, but only a few have succeeded. One of the most infamous and audacious escapes from San Quentin took place in the 20th century, involving a group of convicts who defied all odds and orchestrated a daring break for freedom. This detailed account delves into the history of San Quentin, the circumstances surrounding the escape, the planning and execution of the escape, and the aftermath that followed.

History of San Quentin State Prison

San Quentin's history is as long and storied as the state of California itself. Built during the Gold Rush era, the prison was originally designed to house inmates in conditions that were harsh and punitive. Over the decades, San Quentin became synonymous with criminal notoriety and became one of the most well-known prisons in the United States. It has housed infamous criminals such as Charles Manson, Sirhan Sirhan, and Richard Ramirez, making it a place of fear and legend.

The prison is located on the San Francisco Bay, which makes it naturally secure. Surrounded by water on three sides and fortified with high walls and guard towers, San Quentin was designed to be virtually escape-proof. The harsh conditions, coupled with its isolated location, made it a formidable fortress for anyone attempting to escape.

However, as secure as San Quentin was, it was not impervious to escape attempts. Throughout its history, the prison has seen its fair share of daring and desperate escapes, many of which were foiled by vigilant guards and security measures. Yet, despite the challenges, some convicts were able to exploit weaknesses in the system and orchestrate breakouts that would go down in history.

The Setting: Mid-20th Century San Quentin

The mid-20th century was a turbulent time for San Quentin. The prison population was at an all-time high, and the facility was overcrowded and understaffed. The rise of organized crime, gang activity, and political unrest during this period contributed to a volatile environment within the prison walls. This era also saw an increase in the number of hardened criminals, many of whom were serving life sentences and had little to lose by attempting to escape.

During this time, the prison's security measures were extensive but not infallible. Guard towers, searchlights, armed patrols, and high walls surrounded the facility, but the prison also had its vulnerabilities. The large and ever-growing inmate population meant that guards were often outnumbered, and the sheer size of the prison complex made it difficult to monitor every corner.

The atmosphere within the prison was tense, with frequent clashes between inmates and guards. Prison gangs wielded significant influence, and alliances were often formed based on race and criminal affiliations. It was within this charged environment that the stage was set for one of the most daring escapes in San Quentin's history.

The Masterminds Behind the Escape

The escape from San Quentin was not the result of a spontaneous act of desperation but a meticulously planned operation orchestrated by a group of highly resourceful and determined convicts. The key players in this escape were men who had already spent years behind bars and had little hope of ever seeing freedom through legal means. These inmates were hardened by years of incarceration, and their resolve to break free was unshakeable.

The mastermind behind the escape was a man named George "Tiny" Smith, a career criminal who had been serving a life sentence for armed robbery and murder. Smith was known for his intelligence and resourcefulness, and he had a reputation for being able to manipulate both inmates and guards to his advantage. Despite his nickname, "Tiny" was anything but small in stature; he was a physically imposing figure, standing over six feet tall and weighing more than 200 pounds.

Smith was joined by several other inmates, including Joe "Mad Dog" Sullivan, a notorious hitman with ties to organized crime, and Clarence "Doc" Barker, a member of the infamous Barker-Karpis gang, which had terrorized the Midwest during the 1930s. These men were not only skilled criminals but also highly motivated to escape, as they faced life sentences or the death penalty.

The group of inmates that Smith assembled was carefully chosen for their skills and loyalty. Each member had a specific role to play in the escape plan, from gathering intelligence on prison routines to securing weapons and tools. The group spent months meticulously planning every detail of their escape, leaving nothing to chance.

Planning the Escape

The planning phase of the escape was as critical as the escape itself. The inmates knew that the only way to succeed was to exploit weaknesses in the prison's security system, and they spent months studying the routines of the guards, the layout of the prison, and the schedule of inmate movements.

One of the first steps in their plan was to establish a network of informants and allies within the prison. This network allowed the escapees to gather crucial information about guard shifts, security procedures, and the locations of surveillance cameras. The group also relied on bribery and manipulation to gain the trust of certain guards, who unwittingly provided them with valuable intelligence.

Another key element of the plan was to obtain tools and weapons that would be essential for the escape. Over time, the inmates managed to smuggle in hacksaws, chisels, and makeshift knives, which they used to cut through bars and create a path to freedom. The tools were hidden in the prison's industrial workshop, where inmates worked on various tasks during the day.

One of the most daring aspects of the plan involved creating fake identification documents that would allow the escapees to pass through checkpoints once they were outside the prison walls. The group used stolen materials to forge passes that resembled those used by prison staff, and they practiced using these documents to ensure that they could convincingly pose as guards.

Execution of the Escape Plan

The escape from San Quentin took place on a cold, foggy night, conditions that favored the escapees by reducing visibility and making it more difficult for guards to spot them. The fog also dampened the sound of their movements, allowing them to work quietly and avoid detection.

The escape began in the early hours of the morning, during a shift change when security was at its weakest. The inmates used their smuggled tools to cut through the bars of their cells and made their way to the prison's utility tunnels, which ran beneath the complex. These tunnels provided a hidden route to the outer perimeter of the prison.

Once in the tunnels, the escapees moved quickly and quietly, using their knowledge of the prison's layout to navigate through the maze of pipes and passageways. They avoided detection by timing their movements to coincide with the guard shifts they had carefully studied. The tunnels eventually led them to an area near the prison's industrial yard, where they had previously stashed a makeshift ladder and other equipment.

The group then used the ladder to scale the prison's outer wall, which was one of the most dangerous parts of the escape. The wall was heavily guarded, and searchlights constantly swept the area. However, the fog provided cover, and the escapees were able to climb the wall without being spotted.

Once over the wall, the group made their way to the prison's outer perimeter, where they encountered their first major obstacle: the guard dogs. These highly trained animals were known for their ability to track and apprehend escaping inmates, but the escapees had come prepared. They had smuggled in meat laced with sedatives, which they threw to the dogs to incapacitate them.

With the dogs neutralized, the escapees made their way to the final barrier: the prison's main gate. Here, they used their forged identification documents to pass themselves off as guards, and in the confusion of the foggy night, they were able to walk out of the prison undetected.

The Aftermath: A Manhunt Begins

The escape from San Quentin sent shockwaves through the prison system and the broader public. News of the breakout spread quickly, and authorities launched one of the largest manhunts in California's history to recapture the escapees. Police, state troopers, and the FBI were all mobilized to track down the fugitives, and roadblocks were set up across the state.

The escapees, however, had planned for this eventuality. They split up into smaller groups and went in different directions, making it more difficult for law enforcement to track them. Some headed north toward the mountains, while others made their way south toward Mexico. The group had also arranged for safe houses and contacts in various locations, allowing them to lay low and avoid detection.

Despite their careful planning, the escapees were eventually tracked down, though it took weeks and, in some cases, months. Joe "Mad Dog" Sullivan was the first to be captured after a shootout with police in a small town near the California-Nevada border. Clarence "Doc" Barker was also apprehended after a dramatic chase through the streets of Los Angeles. George "Tiny" Smith, the mastermind of the escape, managed to evade capture for several weeks, but he was eventually cornered in a remote cabin in the Sierra Nevada mountains, where he was arrested after a brief standoff.

The recapture of the escapees brought some relief to the public and the authorities, but it also raised serious questions about the security of San Quentin and the competence of its staff. An investigation was launched to determine how the inmates had been able to orchestrate such a sophisticated escape, and several guards were disciplined or fired as a result.

Impact on San Quentin and Prison Reform

The escape from San Quentin had a profound impact on the prison system, both in California and across the United States. The breakout exposed significant flaws in the security measures at San Quentin, and it led to a comprehensive review of the facility's operations. In the years that followed, San Quentin underwent significant changes, including the installation of more advanced surveillance systems, increased guard training, and the implementation of stricter security protocols.

The escape also prompted broader discussions about prison reform. Critics argued that the overcrowded and understaffed conditions at

San Quentin had contributed to the escape, and they called for improvements in prison management and inmate rehabilitation programs. The incident highlighted the need for better oversight and accountability in the prison system, and it spurred efforts to address the root causes of criminal behavior and reduce recidivism.

In the decades since the escape, San Quentin has continued to be a focal point for discussions about criminal justice and prison reform. The facility remains one of the most well-known prisons in the United States, but it has also become a symbol of the challenges and complexities of the American penal system.

Conclusion: A Daring Breakout and Its Legacy

The escape from San Quentin stands as one of the most daring and well-executed prison breaks in American history. The convicts who orchestrated the escape were highly resourceful and determined, and their actions exposed vulnerabilities in one of the most secure prisons in the country. While the escapees were eventually recaptured, their breakout left a lasting impact on the prison system and highlighted the need for reform.

The legacy of the San Quentin escape is a reminder of the lengths to which individuals will go to achieve freedom, even in the face of seemingly insurmountable odds. It also serves as a cautionary tale about the importance of vigilance, security, and justice in the management of correctional facilities. As we continue to grapple with issues of crime, punishment, and rehabilitation, the story of the San Quentin escape remains a powerful example of the complexities and challenges of the criminal justice system.

Chapter 24: Albert Hicks

Albert W. Hicks, often referred to as the last pirate in New York, was a notorious criminal whose life was filled with crime, murder, and eventual infamy. Born in the early 19th century, Hicks' story is one of brutality, deception, and a daring escape that cemented his place in the annals of criminal history. His life is a testament to the chaotic times in which he lived, where the line between criminality and survival was often blurred.

Early Life and Descent into Crime

Albert Hicks was born around 1820 in Foster, Rhode Island. Little is known about his early life, but it is clear that from a young age, Hicks was drawn to a life of crime. By his own accounts, he had been involved in a variety of criminal activities ranging from theft to piracy. He spent much of his early years wandering up and down the eastern seaboard of the United States, living a life of crime and evading capture by the authorities.

Hicks' criminal activities were not confined to the United States. He was known to have traveled to the West Indies and Central America, where he continued his life of piracy and murder. His crimes were brutal, often involving the murder of entire crews of ships he had boarded. Hicks was a man without a conscience, willing to do whatever it took to get what he wanted.

The E.A. Johnson Incident: The Crime that Sealed His Fate

In 1860, Albert Hicks committed the crime that would eventually lead to his downfall. He boarded a ship called the E.A. Johnson, a small oyster sloop operating in New York Harbor. Hicks had signed on as a crew member under the guise of seeking honest work. However, his true intentions were far more sinister.

One night, while the ship was anchored off the coast of Staten Island, Hicks brutally murdered the captain and the two other crew members with an axe. The murders were particularly gruesome; Hicks did not merely kill his victims but mutilated their bodies in a frenzy of violence. After the murders, Hicks ransacked the ship, taking anything of value before setting the vessel adrift. He then rowed ashore in a small boat, leaving the bloody scene behind.

The next day, the E.A. Johnson was found floating aimlessly in New York Harbor. When authorities boarded the ship, they were horrified by the carnage they found. The bodies of the crew were discovered mutilated and blood-soaked. The news of the brutal murders spread quickly, and a massive manhunt was launched to find the perpetrator.

Capture and Trial: The Beginning of the End

Despite his attempts to cover his tracks, Hicks was captured shortly after the murders. He was found in Providence, Rhode Island, where he had fled after committing the crime. Authorities quickly apprehended him, and he was brought back to New York to stand trial.

The trial of Albert Hicks was a sensation, drawing massive crowds and extensive media coverage. The brutality of the murders and Hicks' own demeanor during the trial captivated the public's attention. Hicks showed no remorse for his crimes, maintaining a cold and indifferent attitude throughout the proceedings.

During the trial, Hicks confessed to the murders but also claimed that he had committed many other crimes throughout his life. He admitted to being a pirate and a murderer, boasting of the many lives he had taken. His confessions only added to the public's fascination with the case.

The trial was swift, and Hicks was found guilty of murder. The judge sentenced him to death, and Hicks was ordered to be hanged. The date of his execution was set for July 13, 1860.

The Infamous Escape Attempt: A Desperate Bid for Freedom

As the date of his execution approached, Hicks made a daring and desperate attempt to escape from his captors. The escape attempt occurred while Hicks was being transported from the courthouse to the Tombs, the notorious Manhattan Detention Complex, where he was being held.

Hicks had managed to smuggle a small file into his cell and had been slowly working to weaken the chains that bound him. On the day of the escape attempt, as he was being led to the Tombs, Hicks saw his opportunity. He overpowered one of the guards, using the weakened chains to his advantage, and made a break for freedom.

The streets of New York were chaotic as news of Hicks' escape spread. People poured into the streets, both out of fear and curiosity, as the authorities scrambled to recapture the infamous criminal. Hicks' escape set off a massive manhunt, with police and vigilantes scouring the city in search of him.

Despite his initial success in escaping custody, Hicks' freedom was short-lived. He was recaptured within hours of his escape attempt, hiding in a warehouse near the waterfront. The authorities quickly subdued him and returned him to the Tombs, where he was placed under even tighter security.

Execution: The Pirate's Final Reckoning

Following his recapture, Hicks' fate was sealed. There would be no further chances for escape. The date of his execution was kept, and on July 13, 1860, Albert Hicks was hanged at the Tombs. The execution was a public spectacle, drawing thousands of spectators who came to witness the death of New York's last pirate.

In his final moments, Hicks maintained his cold demeanor, showing no fear or remorse for his crimes. He reportedly claimed that he was glad to be leaving the world and expressed no regrets about the lives he had taken. His last words were a chilling reminder of the brutal life he had led.

Legacy: The Last Pirate of New York

The story of Albert Hicks did not end with his death. His life and crimes became the subject of numerous books, articles, and even songs. He was immortalized as the last pirate of New York, a figure of both fear and fascination.

Hicks' life serves as a stark reminder of the brutal realities of crime and the thin line between order and chaos in 19th-century America. His escape attempt, though ultimately unsuccessful, added to his legend as a cunning and dangerous criminal who would stop at nothing to achieve his goals.

Today, Albert Hicks is remembered as one of the most notorious criminals in American history. His story is a chilling testament to the dark side of human nature and the consequences of a life lived outside the bounds of law and morality.

Chapter 25: Escape from Rikers Island

Rikers Island, located in the East River between the Bronx and Queens, New York, is one of the most notorious jails in the United States. Over the years, it has housed some of the country's most dangerous criminals and has been synonymous with violence, corruption, and despair. But among the myriad tales of brutality and confinement that emanate from Rikers, few are as gripping as the stories of daring escapes. The notion of breaking out from a high-security facility like Rikers Island seems almost impossible, yet a number of inmates have attempted, and in some cases succeeded, in making their bid for freedom. This narrative delves deep into the history of escape attempts from Rikers Island, detailing the harrowing experiences, ingenuity, and sheer willpower of those who dared to defy the odds.

Rikers Island: A Brief Overview of the Facility

Rikers Island is the largest jail complex in New York City, spanning over 400 acres and comprising multiple facilities. It was first opened in 1932 and has since grown to accommodate thousands of inmates at any given time. The jail complex is infamous for its harsh conditions, including overcrowding, violence among inmates, and allegations of corruption among staff. Over the decades, Rikers has earned a reputation as one of the toughest and most feared jails in America.

The facility is located on an island, making escape seemingly impossible. Surrounded by water and accessible only by a single bridge connected to the Bronx, Rikers Island is designed to keep its inmates securely confined. The island's isolation, coupled with heavy security measures, including high walls, guard towers, and constant surveillance, creates an environment where escape is unthinkable for most.

Yet, despite these formidable barriers, the human spirit's relentless desire for freedom has driven some inmates to attempt the impossible: to escape from Rikers Island.

The Early Escapes: Setting the Precedent

The history of escape attempts from Rikers Island dates back to the early days of the jail's operation. In the mid-20th century, Rikers was already becoming known for its harsh conditions, which pushed some inmates to risk everything for a chance at freedom.

One of the first recorded escape attempts from Rikers occurred in 1957 when three inmates—John Getty, George Whitney, and Charles Duffy—conspired to break free from the island. The trio had managed to fashion makeshift tools and ropes from materials they had secretly collected over several months. Their plan was to scale the prison walls, cross the island, and swim to the mainland. On a dark and foggy night in November, they made their move.

The men successfully climbed the prison walls using their homemade ropes and began their treacherous journey across the island. However, as they approached the shoreline, they were spotted by a guard who immediately raised the alarm. The men, realizing they had been discovered, attempted to swim across the river to the Bronx. Unfortunately for them, the cold November waters and strong currents made the swim nearly impossible. Two of the men, Getty and Whitney, were quickly apprehended by the authorities. The third, Duffy, managed to evade capture for several hours but was eventually found hiding in a nearby marsh.

This early escape attempt, though ultimately unsuccessful, set the stage for future inmates who would seek to challenge the seemingly impenetrable fortress of Rikers Island.

The 1970s: The Decade of Desperation

The 1970s were a turbulent time in New York City, with crime rates soaring and the city's jails, including Rikers Island, becoming overcrowded and increasingly dangerous. The harsh conditions inside the jail, coupled with the growing unrest in the city, fueled a wave of escape attempts during this decade.

One of the most infamous escape attempts of the 1970s occurred in 1973 when four inmates managed to overpower a guard and make their way out of the jail. The inmates, led by Robert Tanner, had been planning the escape for months. Tanner, a convicted armed robber, was the mastermind behind the plan, meticulously studying the jail's routines and identifying the weaknesses in its security.

On the night of the escape, the four men overpowered a guard during a routine check and stole his keys. They quickly made their way to an exit, where they used the keys to unlock the doors leading out of the facility. Once outside, the men sprinted towards the shoreline, where they had previously stashed makeshift rafts constructed from discarded barrels and wooden planks.

The inmates launched their rafts into the East River and began paddling towards the Bronx. However, their escape did not go unnoticed. Guards quickly discovered their absence and alerted the authorities, who launched a massive manhunt. The escapees were eventually spotted by a police helicopter, which guided a patrol boat to their location. The men were captured just a few hundred yards from the Bronx shoreline, their dreams of freedom dashed at the last moment.

The escape attempt was a stark reminder of the desperation felt by many inmates at Rikers Island during this tumultuous period. It also highlighted the lengths to which they were willing to go to escape the brutal conditions of the jail.

The 1980s: The Era of Ingenious Escapes

The 1980s saw a series of escape attempts from Rikers Island that were marked by a level of ingenuity and planning that had not been seen in previous decades. Inmates became more creative in their methods, often exploiting weaknesses in the jail's infrastructure and security measures.

One of the most remarkable escapes of the 1980s occurred in 1985, when a group of inmates managed to break out of Rikers Island by digging a tunnel. The escape was masterminded by James Lucas, a career criminal with a history of bank robberies and jailbreaks. Lucas, who had been incarcerated at Rikers for armed robbery, spent months planning the escape, studying the layout of the jail and gathering a group of like-minded inmates to assist him.

The men began digging a tunnel from their cell block to the outside of the jail complex. They used smuggled tools, including shovels and pickaxes, to excavate the tunnel, carefully disposing of the dirt and debris in the prison yard. The tunnel was dug under the cover of darkness, with the inmates taking turns to work on it in shifts to avoid detection.

After several weeks of digging, the tunnel was complete, stretching over 100 feet from the cell block to a point just outside the jail's perimeter fence. On the night of their escape, the men crawled through the tunnel and emerged on the other side, where they quickly scaled the fence and made their way to the water's edge.

Once again, the East River proved to be a formidable obstacle. The men had prepared for this by constructing a makeshift raft from stolen materials, which they used to attempt to cross the river. However, the raft was poorly constructed and began to take on water shortly after they launched it. The men were forced to abandon the raft and swim for shore, but the strong currents made the swim nearly impossible.

All but one of the inmates were recaptured within hours of their escape. The sole escapee, James Lucas, managed to swim to the Bronx and evade capture for several days before he was apprehended by the authorities. The escape was widely publicized and led to increased security measures at Rikers Island, including the installation of more advanced surveillance systems and the reinforcement of the jail's perimeter.

The 1990s and Beyond: Modern Security Challenges

As the 20th century came to a close, Rikers Island continued to be plagued by escape attempts, though the increasing sophistication of security measures made successful escapes more difficult. The 1990s saw a shift in the tactics used by inmates, who began to rely more on cunning and deception rather than brute force or physical prowess.

One of the most notable escape attempts of the 1990s occurred in 1993, when an inmate named Ralph Barksdale managed to escape by impersonating another prisoner. Barksdale, who had been incarcerated for drug-related offenses, carefully studied the movements and habits of another inmate who was scheduled for release. On the day of the release, Barksdale swapped identification wristbands with the inmate and successfully convinced the guards that he was the one due to be released.

Barksdale was escorted to the jail's processing area, where he was given civilian clothes and released onto the streets of New York City. It was only after the real inmate attempted to leave the facility later that day that the guards realized what had happened. By that time, Barksdale had already disappeared into the city, leaving the authorities scrambling to locate him.

The escape sparked outrage and led to a thorough review of Rikers Island's release procedures. The incident also highlighted the vulnerabilities in the jail's identification processes, prompting the introduction of new measures to prevent similar escapes in the future.

In the years since Barksdale's escape, Rikers Island has continued to face challenges in maintaining security and preventing escape attempts. Despite the implementation of more advanced technology, including biometric identification systems and enhanced surveillance, inmates have continued to find ways to exploit weaknesses in the system.

The High-Profile Escapes: Notorious Cases that Captured National Attention

Among the many escape attempts from Rikers Island, some have stood out for their sheer audacity and the high-profile nature of the inmates involved. These cases have captured national attention and have become part of the lore surrounding the infamous jail.

One such case occurred in 2007, when an inmate named Wayne Doyle attempted to escape from Rikers Island by scaling the jail's 30-foot-high perimeter wall. Doyle, who was awaiting trial for armed robbery, had managed to obtain a length of rope, which he used to climb over the wall. His escape was almost successful; he made it to the other side of the wall and began running towards the water. However, he was spotted by a guard in one of the watchtowers, who immediately sounded the alarm.

A chase ensued, with guards and police officers converging on Doyle as he sprinted towards the shoreline. In a last-ditch effort to evade capture, Doyle jumped into the East River and attempted to swim to the Bronx. The cold water and strong currents quickly took their toll, and Doyle was forced to turn back. He was captured just a few minutes later, shivering and exhausted, having come within inches of freedom.

The escape attempt was widely covered by the media, with many commentators expressing disbelief that an inmate could come so close to escaping from a high-security facility like Rikers Island. The incident led to further scrutiny of the jail's security measures and prompted calls for a comprehensive review of the facility's operations.

Rikers Island Today: Ongoing Challenges and the Future of the Jail

As of the 21st century, Rikers Island remains a focal point of controversy and debate. The facility continues to face significant challenges, including overcrowding, violence, and ongoing security concerns. Despite numerous reforms and improvements, the legacy of escape attempts looms large over the jail's history.

In recent years, there has been growing momentum to close Rikers Island altogether. Advocates for criminal justice reform argue that the jail is beyond redemption and that its closure is necessary to address the systemic issues plaguing New York's criminal justice system. Plans have been proposed to replace Rikers with smaller, borough-based jails that would provide more humane conditions for inmates and reduce the likelihood of escape attempts.

However, as long as Rikers Island remains operational, the specter of escape will continue to haunt the facility. The stories of those who have attempted to break free from the island, whether successful or not, serve as a reminder of the lengths to which individuals will go in pursuit of freedom. These tales are woven into the fabric of Rikers Island's history, contributing to its enduring reputation as one of the most notorious jails in the United States.

Conclusion: The Legacy of Escape from Rikers Island

The history of escape attempts from Rikers Island is a testament to the indomitable human spirit and the relentless pursuit of freedom, even in the face of insurmountable odds. From the early days of the jail's operation to the modern era, inmates have repeatedly tested the limits of the facility's security, using ingenuity, deception, and sheer determination to try and break free.

While the majority of these escape attempts have ended in recapture, they have nonetheless left an indelible mark on the history of Rikers Island. The tales of daring and desperation that have emerged from these incidents serve as a stark reminder of the harsh realities of life inside one of America's most notorious jails.

As Rikers Island faces an uncertain future, with growing calls for its closure, the stories of those who attempted to escape will continue to be remembered as part of the jail's complex and controversial legacy. Whether viewed as acts of defiance, desperation, or sheer audacity, these escape attempts stand as powerful symbols of the human desire for freedom, even in the darkest of circumstances.

Chapter 26: John Boyle O'Reilly

John Boyle O'Reilly was a remarkable figure of the 19th century whose life story is a testament to the power of resilience, intellect, and moral conviction. A man of many talents, O'Reilly was not only a revolutionary and poet but also a journalist, editor, and staunch advocate for social justice. His journey from a young Irish rebel to a revered figure in American society is one of courage, defiance, and an unyielding commitment to the causes he believed in. This detailed account explores the multifaceted life of John Boyle O'Reilly, shedding light on his early years, his involvement in the Irish nationalist movement, his daring escape from an Australian penal colony, and his influential work as a writer and public figure in the United States.

Early Life: The Roots of Rebellion

John Boyle O'Reilly was born on June 28, 1844, in Dowth Castle, County Meath, Ireland, into a family steeped in the rich cultural and political history of Ireland. His father, William David O'Reilly, was a schoolmaster and a devout Catholic, while his mother, Eliza Boyle, came from a lineage of strong-willed and patriotic Irish women. The O'Reilly household was one where education, Irish history, and the struggle for national identity were deeply valued.

From a young age, O'Reilly was exposed to the harsh realities of British rule in Ireland. The Great Famine (1845–1852), which occurred during his early childhood, left a profound impact on him, as he witnessed the suffering and injustices inflicted upon his people. The famine, caused by a devastating potato blight and exacerbated by British policies, led to the death of over a million Irish people and the emigration of another million. These experiences instilled in O'Reilly a deep sense of national pride and a burning desire to see Ireland freed from British oppression.

O'Reilly was an exceptional student, and his intellectual abilities were evident from an early age. He was particularly gifted in languages and literature, which would later serve him well in his career as a writer and poet. By the time he reached his teenage years, O'Reilly was already an ardent nationalist, inspired by the stories of Irish heroes who had fought against British rule.

Joining the Fenians: The Path to Rebellion

In the early 1860s, Ireland was a hotbed of nationalist activity, with various groups advocating for Irish independence. Among the most prominent of these groups was the Irish Republican Brotherhood (IRB), a secret society dedicated to the overthrow of British rule in Ireland. The IRB, more commonly known as the Fenians, was founded in 1858 by James Stephens and quickly gained a substantial following among young Irish men and women.

O'Reilly joined the Fenians in 1863 at the age of 19, driven by his passion for Irish freedom. He became an active member of the organization, using his skills as a writer and speaker to spread the Fenian message. O'Reilly's involvement in the Fenians soon led him to enlist in the British Army, a strategy employed by many Fenians to gain military training and to recruit Irish soldiers to their cause. He joined the 10th Hussars, a cavalry regiment stationed in Ireland, where he began to organize fellow Irish soldiers in preparation for a planned uprising against the British.

However, the Fenian uprising was thwarted before it could begin. In 1866, the British government, having become aware of the Fenian infiltration of its military forces, began arresting suspected members of the IRB. O'Reilly was among those captured and was court-martialed in 1866. He was found guilty of treason and was sentenced to death, a sentence that was later commuted to 20 years of penal servitude.

This commutation likely saved his life, as public opinion in Ireland was increasingly turning against the harsh treatment of Irish nationalists.

Transportation to Australia: The Convict's Fate

After his trial, John Boyle O'Reilly was transported to Australia, a common fate for Irish rebels and criminals during the 19th century. The British Empire used Australia as a penal colony, and many Irish nationalists, including members of the Young Ireland movement and the Fenians, were sent there to serve their sentences in harsh and isolated conditions.

In 1867, O'Reilly was sent aboard the convict ship *Hougoumont* to the Swan River Colony, now known as Western Australia. The journey was long and grueling, lasting several months. The *Hougoumont* was the last ship to transport convicts to Australia, marking the end of an era in British penal history.

Upon arrival in Australia, O'Reilly was assigned to the convict settlement at Bunbury, a small town on the coast of Western Australia. The conditions in the settlement were brutal, with convicts subjected to hard labor, poor rations, and strict discipline. Despite these hardships, O'Reilly maintained his dignity and resolve, using his time in captivity to educate himself further and to plan his escape.

The Great Escape: Freedom from the Chains

John Boyle O'Reilly's escape from Australia is one of the most daring and legendary prison escapes in history. Determined to avoid spending the prime years of his life in bondage, O'Reilly began plotting his escape soon after arriving in Bunbury. He was able to gain the trust of a sympathetic priest, Father Patrick McCabe, who became a crucial ally in his plan to escape.

With the help of Father McCabe and a group of Irish sympathizers in the United States, O'Reilly managed to make contact with the crew of the American whaling ship *Gazelle*, which was operating off the coast of Western Australia. In February 1869, after nearly two years of imprisonment, O'Reilly made his move. He escaped from the convict settlement and, with the help of local Irish settlers, made his way to a remote beach where the *Gazelle* was waiting.

The escape was fraught with danger. O'Reilly had to evade British patrols and navigate the treacherous Australian wilderness. However, his determination and the assistance of the Irish community in Australia ensured his success. Once aboard the *Gazelle*, O'Reilly was hidden by the crew and smuggled out of Australia. The ship then set sail for the United States, a journey that took several months.

O'Reilly arrived in the United States in November 1869, landing in Philadelphia. His successful escape was celebrated by Irish communities around the world, and he was hailed as a hero. O'Reilly's escape not only ensured his own freedom but also inspired other Irish nationalists and cemented his status as a key figure in the Irish struggle for independence.

A New Life in America: Poet, Journalist, and Advocate

After his arrival in the United States, John Boyle O'Reilly quickly established himself as a prominent figure in the Irish-American community. He settled in Boston, Massachusetts, a city with a large Irish population and a strong tradition of Irish nationalism. O'Reilly found work as a journalist, joining the staff of *The Pilot*, a Catholic newspaper that served the Irish-American community.

O'Reilly's talent for writing and his deep commitment to the Irish cause soon made him an influential voice in American journalism. He became the editor of *The Pilot* in 1876, a position he held until his death in 1890. Under his leadership, *The Pilot* became one of the most respected and widely read newspapers in the United States, known for its advocacy of Irish independence, social justice, and civil rights.

As an editor, O'Reilly used his platform to champion a wide range of causes. He was a vocal critic of British rule in Ireland and worked tirelessly to raise awareness of the plight of the Irish people. O'Reilly also became an advocate for the rights of African Americans, Native Americans, and other marginalized groups, reflecting his broader commitment to justice and equality.

In addition to his work as a journalist, O'Reilly was also a gifted poet and author. His poetry, which often explored themes of Irish nationalism, exile, and the longing for freedom, resonated deeply with readers both in the United States and Ireland. His most famous poem, "The Exile of the Gael," captured the pain and pride of the Irish diaspora, while his other works, such as "Songs from the Southern Seas" and "Moondyne," showcased his versatility as a writer.

O'Reilly's literary talents extended beyond poetry. He authored several novels, including *Moondyne*, which was based on his experiences as a convict in Australia. The novel was well-received and further cemented his reputation as a leading literary figure of his time.

The Fenian Movement in America: O'Reilly's Continued Activism

Even after his escape from Australia and his new life in the United States, John Boyle O'Reilly remained deeply involved in the Irish nationalist movement. He became a key figure in the Fenian Brotherhood in America, a sister organization to the Irish Republican Brotherhood. The Fenians in America were dedicated to supporting the cause of Irish independence, often through fundraising, organizing political campaigns, and providing material support to Irish nationalists in Ireland.

O'Reilly's leadership and influence within the Fenian Brotherhood were significant. He used his platform at *The Pilot* to advocate for Irish independence and to rally support for the Fenian cause. O'Reilly was also involved in several high-profile campaigns to secure the release of Irish political prisoners and to raise funds for the Irish nationalist movement.

However, O'Reilly was also a pragmatist, and he recognized the limitations of violent rebellion as a means to achieve Irish independence. Over time, he became more aligned with moderate nationalist movements that sought to achieve independence through political and diplomatic means. O'Reilly's advocacy for a more measured approach to the Irish question earned him both admiration and criticism within the nationalist community.

Despite the challenges and divisions within the movement, O'Reilly remained committed to the cause of Irish freedom until his death. He was a tireless advocate for the rights of the Irish people and played a crucial role in shaping the Irish-American community's response to the struggle for independence.

Legacy: A Life of Courage and Conviction

John Boyle O'Reilly's life was one of extraordinary courage, intellect, and moral conviction. His journey from a young Irish rebel to a respected American writer and advocate for justice is a testament to his resilience and determination. O'Reilly's contributions to the Irish nationalist movement, his literary achievements, and his advocacy for social justice have left an indelible mark on history.

O'Reilly's legacy continues to be celebrated in both Ireland and the United States. In Ireland, he is remembered as a hero of the nationalist movement, a man who risked everything for the cause of Irish freedom.

In the United States, he is honored as a champion of civil rights and a pioneer in the fight for social justice.

Monuments and memorials dedicated to O'Reilly can be found in both countries, including a statue in his honor in Boston, where he spent much of his life. His works continue to be read and studied, offering insight into the struggles and aspirations of the Irish people during a turbulent period in history.

John Boyle O'Reilly's story is a reminder of the power of the human spirit to overcome adversity and to fight for what is right. His life serves as an inspiration to all who seek to make the world a better place, and his legacy as a poet, journalist, and advocate for justice will endure for generations to come.

Chapter 27: Escape from Broadmoor Hospital

The escape from Broadmoor Hospital stands as one of the most audacious and controversial events in the history of psychiatric care in the United Kingdom. Broadmoor, a high-security psychiatric hospital in Berkshire, England, has housed some of the most dangerous and mentally unstable individuals in the country since its establishment in 1863. Despite its stringent security measures and the notorious reputation of its inmates, there have been several escapes from the institution, each shrouded in mystery, fear, and intrigue. The most infamous of these escapes has been the subject of widespread media coverage, governmental inquiries, and public debate. This detailed account delves into the history of Broadmoor Hospital, the circumstances surrounding the escape, the methods used by the escapees, the aftermath, and the broader implications for mental health care and security.

Broadmoor Hospital: The Origins of an Infamous Institution

Broadmoor Hospital, originally known as the Broadmoor Criminal Lunatic Asylum, was established in 1863 to house and treat individuals deemed criminally insane. Located in the village of Crowthorne, Berkshire, the hospital was built in response to the increasing number of individuals who had committed serious crimes but were considered too mentally ill to stand trial or serve a prison sentence. The Victorian era's approach to mental health was a complex blend of compassion and control, and Broadmoor was designed to reflect this duality.

The institution was intended to be both a place of treatment and a secure facility, where patients could receive care for their mental illnesses while being kept away from society. The design of the hospital was based on the "panopticon" model, a concept developed by the philosopher Jeremy Bentham, which allowed for constant surveillance of inmates with minimal staff. The hospital was surrounded by high walls, with wards arranged in a radial pattern to enable easy monitoring of patients.

Over the years, Broadmoor became synonymous with the most notorious and violent criminals in British history. Some of its most infamous inmates included Peter Sutcliffe, the "Yorkshire Ripper"; Ronnie Kray, one half of the notorious Kray twins; and Charles Bronson, one of Britain's most violent prisoners. Despite its fearsome reputation, Broadmoor also became a center for psychiatric research and treatment, with pioneering work done in the fields of forensic psychiatry and criminal psychology.

The Security Measures: A Fortress for the Criminally Insane

Given the nature of its inmates, Broadmoor Hospital was designed with security as a top priority. The hospital's perimeter was fortified with high walls, razor wire, and guard towers, while the internal security was maintained through a combination of locked wards, constant surveillance, and a highly trained staff. The hospital operated on a strict regime, with patients' movements closely monitored and controlled.

Inmates were housed in different wards based on their level of risk and the severity of their mental illness. The most dangerous patients were kept in the highest security wards, where they were subjected to rigorous checks and were rarely allowed to interact with other patients. Visits from family members or legal representatives were conducted under strict supervision, and all communication was closely monitored.

Despite these measures, the very nature of the hospital—housing individuals with severe mental illnesses—posed unique challenges to maintaining security. The staff at Broadmoor had to balance the need for strict control with the ethical responsibility to provide humane and effective treatment. This balancing act created an environment where, despite the best efforts of the authorities, the possibility of escape could never be entirely ruled out.

The Infamous Escapes: A History of Defiance and Evasion

Over its long history, Broadmoor Hospital has seen several escape attempts, some of which were successful and others that were thwarted. Each escape from Broadmoor has sparked widespread public concern, media scrutiny, and debates about the security and management of the institution. The most infamous escape occurred in the early 1950s and involved two patients whose daring and cunning challenged the very foundations of the hospital's security.

One of the most notorious escapes from Broadmoor occurred on January 29, 1952, when two patients, Edwin "Eddie" Boyd and John Straffen, managed to break out of the hospital and evade capture for several hours, causing widespread panic in the local community and beyond.

- **Edwin "Eddie" Boyd: The Mastermind**

Eddie Boyd was a 35-year-old inmate at Broadmoor who had been convicted of armed robbery and was later diagnosed with paranoid schizophrenia. Boyd was known for his intelligence, charm, and manipulative behavior, which had allowed him to gain the trust of some of the hospital staff. Despite his seemingly cooperative demeanor, Boyd harbored a deep resentment towards the authorities and a burning desire to escape from Broadmoor.

Boyd's plan to escape was meticulously calculated. He spent months studying the routines of the staff and identifying weaknesses in the hospital's security measures. Boyd also managed to forge alliances with other inmates, including John Straffen, a 23-year-old convicted murderer who had been found guilty of killing two young girls but was declared insane and committed to Broadmoor.

- **John Straffen: The Accomplice**

John Straffen was one of the most dangerous inmates at Broadmoor. He had a history of violent behavior and had been diagnosed with a severe mental disorder. Straffen's crimes had shocked the nation, and his commitment to Broadmoor was seen as a necessary measure to protect society from his violent tendencies. However, Straffen was also known for his cunning and ability to manipulate those around him, traits that made him a valuable accomplice in Boyd's escape plan.

- **The Escape Plan**

Boyd and Straffen's escape plan was both simple and audacious. Boyd had managed to obtain a key that opened one of the hospital's side gates, likely through manipulation or coercion of a staff member. On the day of the escape, the two men waited for an opportune moment when the staff was preoccupied and security was slightly relaxed.

At around 6:30 PM, Boyd and Straffen made their move. They used the key to unlock the gate and quickly made their way out of the hospital grounds. The duo then scaled the hospital's perimeter wall, using bedsheets tied together as a makeshift rope. Once outside the hospital, they fled into the surrounding countryside, disappearing into the darkness.

The escape was not discovered until several hours later, when a routine check of the wards revealed that Boyd and Straffen were missing. The alarm was immediately raised, and a massive manhunt was launched to capture the escapees. The local community was put on high alert, and police forces from across the region were mobilized to search for the two men.

- **The Aftermath: A Nation in Panic**

The escape of Boyd and Straffen caused widespread panic across the UK. The media sensationalized the story, painting the two men as dangerous lunatics on the loose, and the public was gripped by fear. Parents kept their children indoors, and many residents of the surrounding areas locked their doors and windows, terrified that the escapees might appear at their doorstep.

The manhunt for Boyd and Straffen was one of the largest in British history at the time. Thousands of police officers, supported by the military, scoured the countryside, searching fields, forests, and villages for any sign of the fugitives. The police set up roadblocks, and officers went door to door, warning residents to remain vigilant.

- **The Capture: A Dramatic Conclusion**

The manhunt lasted for several days, during which time Boyd and Straffen managed to evade capture by hiding in the dense woodland surrounding the hospital. However, their luck eventually ran out. On February 1, 1952, Boyd was spotted by a local farmer, who alerted the police. Boyd was captured without incident and returned to Broadmoor, where he was placed in solitary confinement.

Straffen, however, remained at large for several more days, heightening the tension and fear in the community. His capture finally came on February 8, 1952, when he was found hiding in an abandoned barn near the village of Arborfield, approximately 10 miles from Broadmoor. Straffen was also taken back to the hospital, where he was subjected to even stricter security measures.

- **The Fallout: Public Outcry and Institutional Reforms**

The escape of Boyd and Straffen sparked a public outcry and led to a series of inquiries into the security measures at Broadmoor Hospital. The media and the public demanded answers as to how two dangerous individuals could have managed to escape from what was supposed to be a high-security facility. The incident also raised broader questions about the treatment and management of individuals with severe mental illnesses who had committed serious crimes.

The government responded by launching an official inquiry into the escape. The inquiry revealed several lapses in security at Broadmoor, including insufficient supervision of high-risk patients, inadequate staff training, and flaws in the physical security infrastructure of the hospital. The inquiry's findings led to significant changes in the management and security protocols at Broadmoor.

One of the most immediate changes was the installation of more robust physical barriers, including additional fencing, improved lighting, and the construction of new watchtowers. The hospital also implemented stricter procedures for monitoring and controlling the movements of patients, particularly those deemed to be at high risk of escape.

Staff training was also overhauled, with a greater emphasis on security awareness and the management of dangerous individuals. The hospital increased the number of staff on duty at any given time, ensuring that there were always enough personnel to maintain control and supervision of the wards. These changes were designed to prevent any future escapes and to restore public confidence in the institution.

The Broader Implications: Mental Health, Security, and Society

The escape from Broadmoor Hospital had far-reaching implications for the treatment and management of mentally ill individuals within the criminal justice system. It highlighted the complex challenges of balancing the need for security with the ethical obligation to provide humane treatment for those suffering from mental illnesses.

The incident also prompted a national debate about the role of institutions like Broadmoor in society. Some argued that such high-security hospitals were necessary to protect the public from dangerous individuals, while others questioned whether it was appropriate to confine mentally ill individuals in such restrictive and punitive environments.

The escape also underscored the importance of addressing the root causes of criminal behavior in individuals with mental illnesses. It raised questions about the effectiveness of the treatments provided at Broadmoor and whether more could be done to rehabilitate and support patients rather than simply containing them.

In the years following the escape, there were calls for broader reforms in the mental health system, including increased investment in community-based care and the development of alternative forms of treatment for individuals with severe mental illnesses. These discussions laid the groundwork for future changes in the approach to mental health care in the UK.

Conclusion: A Tale of Madness, Defiance, and Change

The escape from Broadmoor Hospital remains one of the most dramatic and controversial events in the history of the UK's criminal justice system. It is a story that encapsulates the tensions between security and care, control and compassion, punishment and rehabilitation. The escape of Eddie Boyd and John Straffen was not just a sensational event; it was a catalyst for change, prompting a reevaluation of how society deals with the most dangerous and vulnerable individuals in its care.

The legacy of the escape continues to influence the way we think about mental health, security, and the criminal justice system. It serves as a reminder of the challenges and responsibilities that come with caring for individuals who are both mentally ill and criminally dangerous. And it is a testament to the enduring struggle to find the right balance between protecting society and providing humane treatment for all individuals, regardless of their mental state.

Chapter 28: Escape from Devil's Island

The escape from Devil's Island is one of the most legendary prison breaks in history, symbolizing the ultimate triumph of human spirit and determination over insurmountable odds. Devil's Island, part of the notorious French penal colony in French Guiana, was a place of despair, where the worst of criminals, political prisoners, and undesirables were sent to live out their days in brutal isolation. Surrounded by shark-infested waters, dense jungle, and treacherous currents, escape from Devil's Island seemed impossible. Yet, the stories of those who dared to defy the odds and flee this hellish prison remain a testament to the indomitable will to survive. This detailed account explores the history of Devil's Island, the conditions faced by prisoners, the famous escapes that captivated the world, and the enduring legacy of this infamous penal colony.

The Creation of Devil's Island: France's Infamous Penal Colony

Devil's Island, or Île du Diable, is one of the three islands that make up the Salvation Islands (Îles du Salut) in French Guiana. The other two islands are Île Royale and Île Saint-Joseph. The French government established the penal colony in 1852 as part of an effort to rid France of its most dangerous and undesirable criminals. The penal colony, officially known as the Bagne de Cayenne, consisted of several prison camps scattered throughout French Guiana, with the most notorious being on the Salvation Islands.

The decision to establish the penal colony in French Guiana was motivated by several factors. The French government sought to relieve overcrowded prisons in France and to deter crime by sending convicts to a remote and inhospitable location. Additionally, the colony was intended to serve as a means of colonization, with the hope that some of the convicts would eventually become settlers in French Guiana.

However, the harsh conditions and the high mortality rate among the prisoners quickly dashed these hopes.

Devil's Island, the smallest and most isolated of the Salvation Islands, was reserved for the most dangerous criminals and political prisoners. It became infamous as a place of no return, where escape was deemed impossible. The island's name alone evoked fear and dread, symbolizing a place of eternal punishment.

Life on Devil's Island: A Living Hell

Life on Devil's Island was a brutal and dehumanizing experience. The prisoners were subjected to harsh and inhumane conditions that tested their physical and mental endurance. The tropical climate, with its intense heat, humidity, and frequent rainstorms, added to the misery of life on the island. Malaria, yellow fever, and other tropical diseases were rampant, and the lack of medical care meant that many prisoners succumbed to illness.

The penal colony operated on a strict and cruel regime. Prisoners were forced to perform hard labor, often in the sweltering heat, with little food or water. The rations provided were meager and barely enough to sustain life. Malnutrition was common, and many prisoners suffered from scurvy and other diseases caused by a lack of proper nutrition. The prisoners were housed in small, overcrowded cells with no ventilation or sanitation, leading to the spread of disease and a high mortality rate.

The psychological torment of life on Devil's Island was as severe as the physical hardships. The isolation and loneliness drove many prisoners to madness. The penal colony was designed to break the spirit of the inmates, and the constant surveillance, beatings, and arbitrary punishments added to the sense of hopelessness. Escape seemed like the only way out, but the island's remote location and the deadly natural barriers made it a daunting prospect.

Despite these conditions, there were those who refused to accept their fate and were determined to escape, no matter the cost.

Famous Escapes: Stories of Defiance and Survival

Over the years, several prisoners attempted to escape from Devil's Island, each story filled with desperation, ingenuity, and courage. While many escape attempts ended in tragedy, a few have become legendary, capturing the imagination of the world.

- **Henri Charrière: The Legend of Papillon**

Perhaps the most famous escape from Devil's Island is that of Henri Charrière, better known by his nickname, Papillon. Charrière's story became widely known after the publication of his autobiography, "Papillon," in 1969, which later became a bestselling book and a successful film. Although some aspects of Charrière's account have been questioned, his tale remains a powerful symbol of resilience and the will to survive.

Henri Charrière was sentenced to life imprisonment in 1931 for the alleged murder of a pimp, a crime he always maintained he did not commit. After being sent to the penal colony in French Guiana, Charrière made several escape attempts, each one more daring than the last. His nickname, Papillon, which means "butterfly" in French, symbolized his desire for freedom.

Charrière's most famous escape attempt occurred in 1944 when he finally managed to flee Devil's Island. Using a bag of coconuts as a makeshift raft, Charrière braved the shark-infested waters and treacherous currents to reach the mainland. His journey to freedom was fraught with danger, but after many trials and tribulations, he eventually made his way to Venezuela, where he was granted asylum.

While the veracity of all the details in Charrière's account has been debated, his story has become legendary, embodying the idea that the human spirit can overcome even the most extreme adversity.

- **Alfred Dreyfus: The Political Prisoner**

Another famous prisoner of Devil's Island was Alfred Dreyfus, a French Jewish army officer who was wrongfully convicted of treason in 1894. The Dreyfus Affair became one of the most significant political scandals in French history, highlighting issues of anti-Semitism, injustice, and corruption within the French military and government.

Dreyfus was sent to Devil's Island in 1895, where he endured years of solitary confinement under grueling conditions. The French government went to great lengths to ensure that Dreyfus could not escape, including building a special hut for him that was constantly guarded by soldiers. Dreyfus was not allowed to communicate with anyone, and his isolation was so severe that he was forbidden to speak, even to his guards.

Unlike other prisoners, Dreyfus never attempted to escape, partly due to the extreme measures taken to prevent it and partly because he believed that the truth would eventually come to light. His faith in justice was eventually vindicated when evidence of his innocence emerged, leading to his exoneration and release in 1899. The Dreyfus Affair had far-reaching consequences, leading to significant reforms in the French military and justice system.

- **The Mass Escape of 1797: A Little-Known Uprising**

One of the earliest and least known escapes from the penal colony occurred in 1797 when a group of convicts staged a daring uprising on Île Royale, one of the islands in the Salvation Islands group. At the time, the penal colony was still in its infancy, and the French government used it primarily as a dumping ground for political prisoners and petty criminals.

The uprising was led by a group of convicts who managed to overpower their guards and seize control of a small boat. The escapees made their way to the mainland, but their newfound freedom was short-lived. Most of the escapees were captured and either killed or recaptured by the French authorities. The leaders of the uprising were executed, and the incident served as a grim reminder of the perils of attempting to escape from the penal colony.

The Treacherous Path to Freedom: The Challenges of Escaping Devil's Island

Escaping from Devil's Island was an almost impossible task, not just because of the physical barriers, but also due to the natural and man-made obstacles that made freedom so elusive.

- **The Shark-Infested Waters**

One of the most formidable barriers to escape was the ocean that surrounded Devil's Island. The waters were infested with sharks, which were drawn to the island by the bodies of dead prisoners that were routinely thrown into the sea. The presence of these predators made any attempt to swim to freedom a deadly proposition. Even those who managed to avoid the sharks had to contend with the powerful currents that swept through the area, making it difficult to reach the mainland.

- **The Dense Jungle**

For those who made it past the treacherous waters, the jungle of French Guiana presented another set of challenges. The dense, impenetrable forest was teeming with dangerous wildlife, including venomous snakes, jaguars, and poisonous insects. The jungle's heat and humidity were oppressive, and the lack of food and clean water meant that many escapees succumbed to hunger and thirst before they could find help.

- **The Hostile Environment**

French Guiana was an inhospitable place, not just because of its natural environment, but also because of the lack of infrastructure and the hostility of the local population. The penal colony was located in a remote area, far from any towns or villages, and the few settlers in the region were often unsympathetic to the plight of the escapees. Many escapees were turned in by locals or recaptured by French soldiers who patrolled the area in search of fugitives.

- **The Ruthless Guards**

The guards at the penal colony were notorious for their brutality and ruthlessness. They were well aware of the dangers of the jungle and the sea and knew that any escape attempt was likely to end in death. Nevertheless, they took every precaution to prevent escapes, including regular patrols, strict surveillance, and harsh punishments for those caught attempting to flee.

Prisoners who were caught trying to escape faced severe consequences, including extended sentences, solitary confinement, and even death. The threat of punishment was meant to deter would-be escapees, but for many prisoners, the hope of freedom was worth the risk.

The Legacy of Devil's Island: A Symbol of Injustice and Human Resilience

Devil's Island was officially closed as a penal colony in 1953, bringing an end to one of the most notorious chapters in the history of the French penal system. Over the course of its 101-year existence, the penal colony claimed the lives of tens of thousands of prisoners, many of whom died from disease, starvation, or the harsh conditions.

The legacy of Devil's Island is a complex one. On one hand, it is a symbol of the brutality and inhumanity of the penal system, a place where individuals were sent to be forgotten, left to die in isolation and despair. On the other hand, it is also a symbol of human resilience, a place where men and women refused to give up hope, even in the face of unimaginable odds.

The stories of those who escaped from Devil's Island have become part of the cultural fabric of the 20th century, inspiring books, films, and legends. The island itself remains a haunting reminder of the past, a place where the ghosts of the past linger, and the memory of those who suffered and died there is preserved.

Today, the ruins of the penal colony serve as a tourist attraction, drawing visitors from around the world who are fascinated by its dark history. The crumbling buildings, rusting chains, and overgrown paths tell the story of a place where the boundaries between civilization and savagery were blurred, where the line between justice and cruelty was often indistinguishable.

In the end, the escape from Devil's Island is more than just a story of a prison break; it is a story of the triumph of the human spirit, a testament to the power of hope and determination in the face of overwhelming adversity. It is a reminder that even in the darkest of places, the light of freedom can never be completely extinguished.

Chapter 29: Escape from Eastern State Penitentiary

Eastern State Penitentiary, located in Philadelphia, Pennsylvania, is one of the most famous and historically significant prisons in the United States. Opened in 1829, it was designed as a revolutionary institution that emphasized solitary confinement and penitence as methods of rehabilitation. The imposing Gothic architecture, with its high walls and fortress-like appearance, was meant to instill fear and awe in those who passed through its gates. However, despite its formidable design and reputation, Eastern State Penitentiary became the site of numerous daring and ingenious escape attempts. This detailed account explores the history of the penitentiary, the conditions that led to its notorious reputation, and the stories of the most remarkable escapes that challenged the prison's security and showcased the unyielding spirit of its inmates.

The Birth of Eastern State Penitentiary: A New Approach to Incarceration

Eastern State Penitentiary was conceived during a time when the American prison system was undergoing significant changes. Prior to its construction, prisons were often overcrowded, unsanitary, and brutal. Punishments were harsh, and prisoners were often subjected to physical abuse and public humiliation. The Quakers, who were influential in the early 19th century, sought to reform the penal system by promoting the idea of penitence, where prisoners would reflect on their crimes in isolation and emerge reformed.

The penitentiary was designed by the British architect John Haviland, who was inspired by the ideas of solitary confinement and penitence. The prison's design was based on the "Pennsylvania System," which emphasized isolation as a means of rehabilitation. Each prisoner was housed in a separate cell, with a small exercise yard attached, and was expected to spend most of their time in solitude, praying and reflecting on their crimes.

The cells were designed to prevent any communication between inmates. They were equipped with a small skylight, known as the "eye of God," which was intended to remind prisoners that they were under constant divine observation. The cell doors were small and low, forcing prisoners to bow their heads as they entered, further emphasizing the idea of penitence.

Eastern State Penitentiary was considered a model prison, and its design and philosophy were adopted by other institutions around the world. However, the harsh conditions and strict enforcement of solitary confinement led to significant psychological distress among the inmates. The isolation, combined with the monotony of prison life, drove many prisoners to despair, and the penitentiary quickly earned a reputation as a place of suffering.

Life Inside the Walls: The Harsh Reality of Eastern State Penitentiary

Despite its noble intentions, life inside Eastern State Penitentiary was anything but rehabilitative. The prison's strict regime of solitary confinement, combined with the lack of human interaction, took a severe toll on the mental and physical health of the inmates. Many prisoners experienced extreme loneliness, depression, and even madness as a result of their prolonged isolation.

The cells were small, measuring just 8 by 12 feet, with a narrow bed, a toilet, and a small desk. The only light came from the skylight, and prisoners were forbidden from decorating their cells or having any personal belongings. They were allowed to work in their cells, performing tasks such as shoemaking or weaving, but were not allowed to speak or communicate with anyone.

The silence was strictly enforced, and any violation of the rules was met with severe punishment. Guards patrolled the corridors wearing woolen socks over their shoes to muffle their footsteps, and prisoners were required to wear hoods over their heads when being moved around the prison to prevent them from seeing or interacting with others. The isolation was so intense that some inmates developed a condition known as "prison psychosis," characterized by hallucinations, paranoia, and other symptoms of mental illness.

While some prisoners accepted their fate and endured their sentences in silence, others began to plot their escape. The oppressive conditions, combined with the natural human desire for freedom, led to a number of daring and ingenious escape attempts, many of which have become legendary.

The Great Escape of 1945: Clarence Klinedinst and William Russell

One of the most famous escape attempts from Eastern State Penitentiary occurred in 1945, when two inmates, Clarence Klinedinst and William Russell, orchestrated a meticulously planned breakout that captured the attention of the nation. Their escape, which involved tunneling out of the prison over several months, became one of the most daring and successful prison breaks in American history.

- **The Mastermind: Clarence Klinedinst**

Clarence Klinedinst was serving a long sentence for robbery when he began to devise a plan to escape from Eastern State Penitentiary. A skilled and resourceful man, Klinedinst was determined to regain his freedom, despite the formidable barriers that stood in his way. He began to carefully study the layout of the prison, paying close attention to the construction of the walls, the positioning of the guards, and the routines of the prison staff.

Klinedinst's plan was ambitious: he would dig a tunnel from his cell to the outside of the prison walls, using only the limited tools and materials available to him. To accomplish this, he enlisted the help of another inmate, William Russell, who was serving time for burglary. Together, the two men began to work on their escape, using spoons, pieces of metal, and other makeshift tools to dig the tunnel.

- **The Tunnel: A Feat of Ingenuity**

The construction of the tunnel was a painstaking and dangerous process. Klinedinst and Russell worked on the tunnel at night, after the guards had completed their rounds. They carefully concealed the entrance to the tunnel, which was located beneath a loose stone in the floor of Klinedinst's cell. Each night, they would dig a few inches of the tunnel, using spoons and metal scraps to chip away at the dirt and rock.

The tunnel had to be deep enough to avoid detection and long enough to reach beyond the prison walls. To prevent the tunnel from collapsing, the men used pieces of wood and other materials to reinforce the walls and ceiling. They also had to find a way to dispose of the dirt they excavated, which they did by spreading it thinly across the floor of their cells or flushing it down the toilet in small amounts.

The tunnel eventually extended over 100 feet, passing beneath the prison yard and the perimeter wall. The men worked tirelessly for several months, driven by the hope of freedom and the fear of discovery. Despite the constant risk of being caught, they remained undeterred, their determination growing stronger with each passing day.

- **The Breakout: A Daring Escape**

On the night of April 3, 1945, Klinedinst and Russell made their move. After completing their final preparations, they crawled through the tunnel, emerging outside the prison walls in a nearby field. From there, they quickly fled the area, disappearing into the night before the prison authorities even realized they were gone.

The escape was a shocking and embarrassing failure for the prison, which had been considered one of the most secure in the country. A massive manhunt was launched to recapture the fugitives, but Klinedinst and Russell managed to evade capture for several weeks. Their escape became front-page news, and the public followed the story with intense interest, fascinated by the ingenuity and audacity of the two men.

Eventually, both Klinedinst and Russell were recaptured and returned to Eastern State Penitentiary, where they were placed in solitary confinement as punishment for their escape. However, their daring breakout became a part of prison lore, inspiring future generations of inmates to attempt their own escapes.

Willie Sutton: The Gentleman Bank Robber and His Multiple Escapes

Another notorious figure associated with Eastern State Penitentiary is Willie Sutton, one of the most famous bank robbers in American history. Known as the "Gentleman Bandit" for his polite and non-violent approach to crime, Sutton became a legend in the criminal underworld for his numerous successful bank heists and his repeated escapes from custody.

- **The Early Years: A Life of Crime**

Willie Sutton was born in Brooklyn, New York, in 1901. He grew up in poverty and turned to crime at an early age, committing his first robbery at the age of 18. Over the next several years, Sutton became a master of disguise and a skilled thief, robbing banks across the country and amassing a small fortune in stolen money.

Sutton's criminal career was marked by his ability to evade capture, often escaping from custody shortly after being arrested. His charm and wit endeared him to the public, who viewed him as a modern-day Robin Hood, stealing from the rich and eluding the authorities with style.

- **Sutton's First Escape from Eastern State Penitentiary**

Willie Sutton was first imprisoned at Eastern State Penitentiary in 1934 after being convicted of multiple bank robberies. However, his time at the penitentiary was short-lived, as he quickly began to plot his escape. Using his skills as a master of disguise and his ability to manipulate others, Sutton managed to escape from the prison in 1934, just a few months after his arrival.

Sutton's first escape involved tricking a prison guard into believing that he was an inmate who had been granted permission to leave the prison. Disguised as a civilian, Sutton simply walked out of the prison gates and disappeared into the streets of Philadelphia. The escape was a major embarrassment for the prison authorities, who were left scrambling to explain how one of the most notorious criminals in the country had managed to walk out of their custody.

- **The 1945 Escape: A Masterful Breakout**

After being recaptured and sentenced to life in prison, Willie Sutton was once again sent to Eastern State Penitentiary in 1945. However,

Sutton was not content to spend the rest of his life behind bars, and he quickly began planning his next escape.

This time, Sutton enlisted the help of several other inmates, including Clarence Klinedinst, who had recently completed his own escape attempt. The group of prisoners began working on a new tunnel, similar to the one used by Klinedinst and Russell, with the goal of escaping through the prison's drainage system.

The escape plan was meticulously planned, with each inmate assigned a specific task. Sutton used his skills as a master of disguise to create fake identification documents and uniforms, which the prisoners planned to use once they were outside the prison walls. The group worked tirelessly on the tunnel, digging it out of the prison's laundry room and extending it beneath the prison yard.

On February 10, 1945, Sutton and his fellow inmates made their escape. They crawled through the tunnel, emerging in a nearby field, and quickly fled the area. The escape was another major embarrassment for the prison, which had once again been outsmarted by Sutton and his accomplices.

However, Sutton's freedom was short-lived. He was recaptured just a few months later, after a tip from an informant led the police to his hideout in Brooklyn. Despite his repeated escapes, Sutton was eventually sentenced to life in prison, where he remained until his death in 1980.

The Legacy of Eastern State Penitentiary: A Monument to Crime and Punishment

Eastern State Penitentiary closed its doors in 1971, after more than 140 years of operation. The prison, once considered a model of reform, had become a symbol of the failures of the American penal system. The harsh conditions, combined with the numerous escape attempts, exposed the flaws in the prison's design and philosophy, leading to calls for its closure.

Today, the penitentiary stands as a National Historic Landmark, preserved as a museum and tourist attraction. The crumbling walls, rusting cell doors, and overgrown courtyards serve as a haunting reminder of the prison's dark past. Visitors can explore the cells, learn about the history of the prison, and hear the stories of the inmates who once called Eastern State Penitentiary home.

The escape attempts from Eastern State Penitentiary have become the stuff of legend, inspiring books, movies, and television shows. The stories of Willie Sutton, Clarence Klinedinst, and William Russell, among others, continue to captivate the public's imagination, serving as a testament to the ingenuity and determination of those who refused to be confined.

In the end, the escape from Eastern State Penitentiary is more than just a series of daring prison breaks; it is a story of human resilience, a reminder that the desire for freedom can never be fully extinguished, even in the most oppressive of environments. The legacy of Eastern State Penitentiary lives on, not just in the walls of the prison itself, but in the stories of those who dared to defy the odds and seek their own path to freedom.

Chapter 30: Escape from Robben Island

Robben Island, located in Table Bay off the coast of Cape Town, South Africa, is one of the most infamous prison islands in the world. Its history is inextricably linked with the story of apartheid in South Africa, as it was here that many of the country's most prominent political prisoners, including Nelson Mandela, were incarcerated during the apartheid era. Over the centuries, Robben Island has served as a leper colony, a mental institution, and, most notoriously, as a maximum-security prison. The island's isolation, surrounded by frigid waters and dangerous currents, made it an almost inescapable fortress. Yet, throughout its long and brutal history, there were daring attempts to escape its confines. This detailed account explores the history of Robben Island, the harrowing conditions of life there, and the stories of those who attempted the seemingly impossible: to escape from Robben Island.

Robben Island: From Remote Outpost to Political Prison

Robben Island's name, derived from the Dutch word for "seals" (robben), reflects its early history as a remote outpost used by Dutch settlers in the 17th century. Initially, the island served as a place of exile, where political prisoners, social outcasts, and those considered dangerous were sent to live out their days in isolation. The first recorded prisoner on Robben Island was Autshumato, a Khoikhoi leader who was exiled there in 1658 for resisting Dutch colonization. This began the island's long history as a place of punishment and banishment.

In the centuries that followed, Robben Island was used as a leper colony and a mental asylum. The harsh conditions, combined with the island's isolation, made it a dreaded place, feared by those who knew they might be sent there. However, it was during the 20th century, particularly under the apartheid regime, that Robben Island became internationally notorious as a prison for political dissidents and activists.

The Apartheid Era: Robben Island as a Maximum-Security Prison

In 1961, during the height of apartheid in South Africa, Robben Island was transformed into a maximum-security prison for political prisoners. The island became a symbol of the apartheid government's brutality and repression, as many of South Africa's most prominent anti-apartheid leaders were imprisoned there. Among the most famous inmates was Nelson Mandela, who was incarcerated on the island for 18 of his 27 years in prison.

The conditions on Robben Island during the apartheid era were deliberately harsh and dehumanizing. Prisoners were subjected to forced labor, breaking rocks in a limestone quarry under the blistering sun. They were housed in small, damp cells with minimal provisions, and were constantly surveilled by prison guards who enforced strict rules and brutal punishments. Communication with the outside world was severely limited, and prisoners were denied basic rights, including adequate food, medical care, and legal representation.

The apartheid government's intention was clear: to break the spirits of those who dared to challenge its authority. However, the prisoners on Robben Island, many of whom were leaders of the African National Congress (ANC) and other anti-apartheid organizations, refused to be broken. Despite the isolation and brutality, they continued to resist, organizing clandestine meetings, educating one another, and maintaining their resolve to fight for freedom and justice.

The Challenges of Escaping Robben Island

Escaping from Robben Island was considered virtually impossible. The island is located about 7 kilometers (4.3 miles) from the mainland, surrounded by the cold, shark-infested waters of the Atlantic Ocean. The treacherous currents and strong winds made swimming to freedom a near-suicidal endeavor. The prison itself was heavily fortified, with armed guards, barbed wire fences, and high walls designed to prevent any escape attempts.

The prisoners on Robben Island were constantly monitored, and the strict regimen of work and confinement left little opportunity for planning an escape. Any attempt to escape would require not only extraordinary courage and determination but also meticulous planning and the ability to overcome the island's natural and man-made defenses.

Yet, despite these formidable challenges, there were several daring attempts to escape from Robben Island. These attempts, though often unsuccessful, have become legendary, symbolizing the unbreakable spirit of those who refused to accept their fate.

The 1961 Escape Attempt: The Tale of Harold Strachan and Anthony Figaji

One of the earliest and most audacious escape attempts from Robben Island occurred in 1961, shortly after the island was converted into a maximum-security prison. The escape was orchestrated by two political prisoners, Harold Strachan and Anthony Figaji, who were determined to break free from the island's confines.

- **The Mastermind: Harold Strachan**

Harold Strachan was a former World War II pilot and a member of the ANC's military wing, Umkhonto we Sizwe (MK). He was arrested and sentenced to six years in prison for his involvement in sabotage activities against the apartheid government. Strachan was known for his resourcefulness and his willingness to take risks, qualities that would prove essential in his escape attempt.

- **The Escape Plan: A Daring Scheme**

Strachan and Figaji devised a plan to escape from Robben Island by stealing a boat from the prison's harbor. The plan was fraught with risks: they would have to evade the guards, avoid detection by the island's patrols, and navigate the treacherous waters of the Atlantic Ocean to reach the mainland. The two men spent weeks observing the guards' routines and the layout of the harbor, carefully planning their escape.

On the night of their escape, Strachan and Figaji made their way to the harbor, where they found a small boat. They managed to start the engine and set off towards the mainland, but their plan quickly unraveled. The rough seas and strong currents made it nearly impossible to navigate the boat, and they soon realized they were not going to make it. Rather than risk being recaptured and facing severe punishment, the two men decided to turn back.

When they returned to the island, they were caught and severely punished for their escape attempt. Despite the failure of their plan, Strachan and Figaji's daring attempt became a symbol of the determination and bravery of those who were imprisoned on Robben Island. Their story was a reminder that, even in the face of overwhelming odds, the desire for freedom could not be extinguished.

The 1965 Escape Attempt: The Ingenious Plot of Stephen Lee and Alex Moumbaris

In 1965, another daring escape attempt was made by two political prisoners, Stephen Lee and Alex Moumbaris, who were also members of Umkhonto we Sizwe. Both men were committed anti-apartheid activists, and their imprisonment on Robben Island only strengthened their resolve to continue the fight for freedom.

- **The Plot: An Ingenious Plan**

Lee and Moumbaris knew that escaping from Robben Island would require more than just courage; it would require an ingenious plan that could outsmart the island's formidable defenses. The two men spent months carefully planning their escape, studying the layout of the prison, the routines of the guards, and the tides and currents around the island.

Their plan involved escaping through the prison's drainage system, which they believed would lead them to the shore. Once outside the prison walls, they intended to swim to a small nearby island, from where they could signal for help or attempt to swim to the mainland. It was a risky plan, but it was their best chance of escaping the island's clutches.

- **The Execution: A Daring Attempt**

On the night of their escape, Lee and Moumbaris made their way to the drainage system, where they managed to pry open a grate and enter the tunnel. The narrow, dark passage was filled with sewage, and the men had to crawl through it for several hundred meters to reach the exit. The journey was harrowing, but they managed to make it to the end of the tunnel, where they emerged near the shore.

Once outside, the men were faced with the daunting task of swimming through the cold, rough waters of the Atlantic Ocean. They knew that the odds were against them, but they were determined to make it to freedom. Unfortunately, their escape attempt was discovered before they could make it to the water, and they were quickly recaptured by the prison guards.

Despite their failure, Lee and Moumbaris' escape attempt was celebrated as a bold and courageous act of defiance. Their willingness to risk their lives for the chance of freedom inspired other prisoners and became part of the island's rich history of resistance.

The 1969 Escape Attempt: The Dramatic Flight of Cedric Mayson

One of the most dramatic escape attempts from Robben Island occurred in 1969, when Cedric Mayson, a prominent anti-apartheid activist and member of the South African Communist Party, made a daring bid for freedom. Mayson's escape attempt was marked by its audacity and the intense manhunt that followed.

• The Escape Plan: A Desperate Gamble

Mayson was determined to escape from Robben Island, despite the near-impossible odds. His plan involved scaling the prison walls and making his way to the island's shoreline, where he would attempt to swim to the mainland. Mayson knew that the chances of success were slim, but he was willing to take the risk in order to regain his freedom.

On the night of his escape, Mayson used a makeshift rope made from bedsheets to scale the prison walls. He then made his way through the prison's outer perimeter and reached the shore. From there, he dove into the icy waters of the Atlantic Ocean and began swimming towards the mainland.

• The Manhunt: A Race Against Time

Mayson's escape was quickly discovered, and the authorities launched a massive manhunt to capture him. Patrol boats and helicopters were dispatched to search the waters around Robben Island, while the police scoured the coastline for any sign of the fugitive. The search was intense, as the apartheid government was determined to recapture Mayson and prevent any further escapes from the island.

Mayson managed to evade capture for several hours, swimming through the frigid waters and using his knowledge of the currents to stay ahead of the search teams. However, his strength eventually began to wane, and he was forced to seek refuge on a small rocky outcrop near the island. Exhausted and suffering from hypothermia, Mayson was eventually spotted by a patrol boat and taken back to Robben Island.

Despite his capture, Mayson's escape attempt was hailed as a remarkable act of bravery. His determination to defy the apartheid regime, even at the risk of his own life, made him a hero among his fellow prisoners and a symbol of resistance against oppression.

The 1971 Escape Attempt: The Unfinished Tunnel of John Harris

In 1971, another daring escape attempt was made by John Harris, a member of the African Resistance Movement (ARM), who had been imprisoned on Robben Island for his involvement in a bombing campaign against the apartheid government. Harris's escape plan involved digging a tunnel from his cell to the island's shoreline, a project that would take months to complete.

- **The Tunnel: A Labor of Determination**

Harris was determined to escape from Robben Island, despite the enormous challenges involved. He spent months digging a tunnel from his cell, using makeshift tools and working in secret to avoid detection by the prison guards. The tunnel, which was painstakingly dug through the island's rocky soil, was intended to reach the shore, where Harris would attempt to swim to freedom.

- **The Discovery: A Plan Foiled**

Despite Harris's best efforts, his escape plan was discovered before he could complete the tunnel. The prison guards, who had become suspicious of Harris's activities, conducted a search of his cell and found the entrance to the tunnel. Harris was immediately placed in solitary confinement, and the tunnel was filled in to prevent any further escape attempts.

Although Harris's escape attempt was ultimately unsuccessful, it was a testament to his determination and ingenuity. His willingness to undertake such a difficult and dangerous project, despite the overwhelming odds, inspired other prisoners on Robben Island and became part of the island's legendary history of resistance.

The Legacy of Robben Island: A Symbol of Resistance and Freedom

The escape attempts from Robben Island, though often unsuccessful, are a testament to the unbreakable spirit of those who were imprisoned there. These attempts, marked by extraordinary courage, determination, and ingenuity, have become part of the island's rich history of resistance against oppression.

Robben Island itself has become a symbol of the struggle for freedom in South Africa. After the end of apartheid, the island was declared a National Heritage Site, and it is now a museum and a symbol of the country's painful past and its triumph over injustice. The stories of those who attempted to escape from Robben Island serve as a reminder of the resilience of the human spirit and the enduring desire for freedom, even in the face of seemingly insurmountable odds. Today, Robben Island stands not just as a reminder of the brutalities of apartheid, but also as a beacon of hope and a testament to the power of resistance and the quest for justice.

Chapter 31: Escape from Sing Sing

Sing Sing, one of the most notorious prisons in American history, has long held a reputation for its strict security, infamous inmates, and dramatic escape attempts. Located in Ossining, New York, the prison has been the site of countless stories of crime and punishment since its establishment in 1826. Among these stories are those of daring escapes—tales that highlight the lengths to which some prisoners would go to break free from the confines of one of the most feared institutions in the country. This detailed exploration delves into the history of Sing Sing, its most infamous escape attempts, and the broader context of life behind its walls.

The History of Sing Sing Prison: A Fortress of Punishment

Sing Sing, named after the Native American Sinck Sinck tribe, was established in 1826 as part of New York State's prison system. The prison was constructed using stone quarried by inmates themselves, and its design was influenced by the Auburn system, which emphasized strict discipline, silence, and hard labor. Sing Sing quickly became known for its harsh conditions, with prisoners subjected to long hours of work, brutal punishments, and minimal contact with the outside world.

The prison's early years were marked by a strict regimen of labor, with inmates toiling in the quarry and various workshops. The philosophy behind this approach was that hard work would instill discipline and reform in the prisoners. However, the reality was often one of exploitation, with prisoners subjected to grueling conditions and harsh punishments for any infraction.

Over the years, Sing Sing became infamous for its death row, where hundreds of inmates were executed in the electric chair. The phrase "sent up the river" became synonymous with being sent to Sing Sing, reflecting the fear and dread associated with the prison. Despite its reputation as an impenetrable fortress, there have been several daring escape attempts throughout its history—each one a testament to the ingenuity and determination of those who refused to accept their fate.

The Challenges of Escaping Sing Sing

Escaping from Sing Sing was no easy feat. The prison was designed to be a fortress, with high walls, guard towers, and a strict regime that left little room for error. Inmates were closely monitored, and any attempt to escape was met with severe punishment. The prison's location on the banks of the Hudson River added an additional layer of difficulty, as would-be escapees would have to navigate the treacherous waters to reach freedom.

The prison's layout, with its cellblocks, workshops, and yards, was designed to minimize the possibility of escape. Guards were stationed at key points throughout the facility, and regular headcounts ensured that any missing inmate would be quickly noticed. In addition to the physical barriers, the psychological toll of imprisonment in Sing Sing was immense, with many inmates succumbing to despair and hopelessness.

Despite these formidable challenges, there were several instances in which prisoners managed to escape—or at least make a valiant attempt. These stories, though often ending in recapture or death, highlight the desperation and resourcefulness of those who sought to break free from Sing Sing's grip.

The 1865 Escape: The Audacious Plot of Bill Minor

One of the earliest and most audacious escape attempts from Sing Sing occurred in 1865, when William "Bill" Minor, a notorious river pirate and gang leader, managed to break free from the prison. Minor, who had been sentenced to life in Sing Sing for his role in a series of violent crimes, was determined not to spend the rest of his days behind bars.

- **The Mastermind: Bill Minor**

Bill Minor was a feared figure along the Hudson River, known for his involvement in piracy, robbery, and murder. His capture and conviction were celebrated as a major victory for law enforcement, and his sentence to Sing Sing was intended to put an end to his criminal activities. However, Minor was not content to simply serve out his sentence; he began planning his escape almost as soon as he arrived at the prison.

- **The Escape Plan: Exploiting a Weakness**

Minor's escape plan involved exploiting a weakness in the prison's security—a gap in the perimeter fence near the prison's dockyard. Minor knew that the prison guards were less vigilant in this area, and he began to devise a plan to use the river as his means of escape. With the help of several accomplices on the outside, Minor arranged for a boat to be waiting for him near the dockyard.

On the night of his escape, Minor managed to slip away from his work detail and make his way to the dockyard. He used the cover of darkness to avoid detection by the guards and made his way to the waiting boat. Once on board, he and his accomplices quickly rowed away from the prison, using the strong current of the Hudson River to their advantage.

- **The Aftermath: A Brief Taste of Freedom**

Minor's escape was a major embarrassment for the prison authorities, who launched a massive manhunt to recapture him. Despite their efforts, Minor managed to evade capture for several weeks, using his knowledge of the river and its surrounding areas to stay one step ahead of the law. However, his freedom was short-lived; he was eventually recaptured after a fierce gunfight with the police and returned to Sing Sing, where he was placed in solitary confinement as punishment for his escape.

Despite the ultimate failure of his escape, Bill Minor's daring attempt became part of the lore of Sing Sing, illustrating the lengths to which some prisoners would go to regain their freedom.

The 1926 Escape: The Ingenious Tunnel of James Watson and His Accomplices

In 1926, Sing Sing was the site of one of the most ingenious escape attempts in its history, when James Watson and several of his fellow inmates managed to dig a tunnel from the prison's workshop to the outside world. The escape, which was meticulously planned and executed, is remembered as one of the most remarkable feats of engineering ever attempted by prisoners.

- **The Mastermind: James Watson**

James Watson, a career criminal with a history of bank robberies and burglaries, was serving a lengthy sentence at Sing Sing when he began planning his escape. Watson was known for his intelligence and resourcefulness, and he quickly realized that the only way to escape the prison would be to go underground—literally.

- **The Tunnel: A Feat of Engineering**

Watson and his accomplices began digging a tunnel from the prison's workshop, where they worked during the day. The workshop was located near the prison's outer wall, making it an ideal location to start the tunnel. The prisoners worked in shifts, using stolen tools and makeshift equipment to dig through the earth and rock.

The tunnel was carefully designed to avoid detection, with the entrance hidden beneath a workbench in the workshop. The prisoners used a system of pulleys and ropes to remove the dirt and debris from the tunnel, which they disposed of in the prison's yard. The tunnel was reinforced with wooden supports to prevent it from collapsing, and the prisoners took great care to avoid making any noise that might alert the guards.

- **The Escape: A Daring Break for Freedom**

After several months of digging, the tunnel was finally completed, and the prisoners were ready to make their escape. On the night of the escape, Watson and his accomplices slipped into the tunnel and made their way to the outside world. The tunnel led them to a wooded area near the prison, where they emerged undetected.

Once outside, the prisoners scattered in different directions, hoping to avoid capture. Watson managed to make it several miles from the prison before he was eventually caught by a passing police patrol. His accomplices were also captured over the following days, and all were returned to Sing Sing to face punishment for their escape.

Despite the failure of their escape, Watson and his accomplices' tunnel remains one of the most remarkable feats of engineering ever attempted by prisoners. Their ingenuity and determination to escape from one of the most secure prisons in the country became a legend in the annals of Sing Sing's history.

The 1941 Escape Attempt: The Story of John Resko and Paul Petrillo

The 1941 escape attempt by John Resko and Paul Petrillo is another of Sing Sing's most famous breakouts. This escape attempt was notable not only for its boldness but also for the dramatic events that unfolded during the prisoners' brief taste of freedom.

- **The Prisoners: John Resko and Paul Petrillo**

John Resko and Paul Petrillo were both serving life sentences at Sing Sing for murder. Resko, a career criminal, had been convicted of killing a storekeeper during a botched robbery, while Petrillo was a member of the infamous "Murder, Inc." gang, responsible for numerous contract killings.

- **The Escape Plan: A Violent Breakout**

Resko and Petrillo's escape plan involved overpowering a guard and stealing his keys to unlock the prison gate. The two men had spent weeks studying the guards' routines and identifying a vulnerable moment when they could strike. On the night of their escape, they put their plan into action.

Using a homemade weapon, Resko and Petrillo attacked a guard who was patrolling near the prison gate. They managed to subdue him and take his keys, which they used to unlock the gate and make their way outside. The escape was a success, and the two men quickly fled into the nearby woods, where they hoped to evade capture.

- **The Manhunt: A Deadly Game of Cat and Mouse**

The escape of Resko and Petrillo triggered a massive manhunt, with law enforcement agencies from across the state mobilizing to capture the fugitives. The two men managed to stay hidden for several days, moving from one hiding place to another and relying on their criminal instincts to avoid detection.

However, their freedom was short-lived. After several days on the run, Resko and Petrillo were spotted by a police patrol, leading to a dramatic chase and shootout. Petrillo was killed in the ensuing gunfight, while Resko was captured and returned to Sing Sing. The escape attempt ended in tragedy, but it became one of the most notorious episodes in the prison's history.

The Legacy of Escape Attempts at Sing Sing

The various escape attempts from Sing Sing, though often unsuccessful, are a testament to the human spirit's desire for freedom, even in the face of seemingly insurmountable odds. The prisoners who attempted to escape from Sing Sing were often motivated by desperation, a refusal to accept their fate, and a willingness to risk everything for a chance at freedom.

Sing Sing itself remains one of the most storied prisons in American history, with a legacy that includes not only its infamous inmates and executions but also the daring escapes that have become part of its mythos. The stories of those who attempted to escape from Sing Sing serve as a reminder of the extreme conditions that can drive individuals to extraordinary lengths in their quest for freedom.

Chapter 32: Escape from Shawshank

The phrase "Escape from Shawshank" immediately conjures images of one of the most famous and gripping prison escape stories ever told, immortalized in Stephen King's novella *Rita Hayworth and Shawshank Redemption* and its acclaimed film adaptation *The Shawshank Redemption*. Although fictional, the story of Andy Dufresne's escape from Shawshank State Penitentiary is celebrated for its cleverness, endurance, and the profound message of hope against all odds. In this comprehensive exploration, we'll delve deeply into the narrative of Shawshank's escape, examining the intricate planning, the harrowing experiences, and the powerful themes that have made this tale a timeless symbol of resilience and redemption.

The Setting: Shawshank State Penitentiary

Shawshank State Penitentiary, the setting for this legendary escape, is depicted as a grim and oppressive institution in Maine, where inmates live under the thumb of corrupt officials and a brutal regime. The prison is characterized by its towering stone walls, dimly lit corridors, and an atmosphere of despair that permeates the lives of its inhabitants. For many inmates, Shawshank is not just a prison but a place where hope comes to die.

The institution is governed by Warden Samuel Norton, a man who outwardly portrays himself as a pious and upstanding citizen but is, in reality, deeply corrupt and ruthless. Norton's regime at Shawshank is marked by exploitation, with prisoners used as cheap labor for the warden's illicit schemes. The guards, led by the sadistic Captain Byron Hadley, enforce the warden's rule with violence and intimidation, ensuring that any hope of escape is snuffed out before it can even begin.

Shawshank is a place where time seems to stand still, where years blur into decades, and where the inmates, many of whom are serving life sentences, struggle to find meaning or purpose in their existence. The pervasive sense of hopelessness is a central theme in the story, setting the stage for one of the most remarkable escapes ever conceived.

Andy Dufresne: The Man Who Defied the Odds

At the heart of the story is Andy Dufresne, a former banker who is wrongfully convicted of the murder of his wife and her lover. Sentenced to two consecutive life terms at Shawshank, Andy quickly becomes an enigmatic figure within the prison. Unlike many of his fellow inmates, Andy refuses to succumb to the despair that defines life at Shawshank. Instead, he maintains a quiet dignity and a steadfast belief in his own innocence, which sets him apart from the other prisoners.

Andy's background as a banker becomes a crucial element of his survival strategy. Early on, he offers his financial expertise to the guards, helping them navigate tax issues and manage their finances. This earns him some protection and privileges within the prison, but it also draws him deeper into the corrupt world of Warden Norton's schemes. Over time, Andy becomes indispensable to the warden, helping him launder money through various fraudulent enterprises. This dual role—as both a prisoner and a tool of corruption—places Andy in a precarious position, but it also provides him with unique opportunities to plan his escape.

The Planning: Years of Quiet Preparation

Andy's escape from Shawshank is the result of years of meticulous planning, patience, and unwavering determination. Unlike many prison escapes that rely on brute force or sudden opportunities, Andy's plan is a slow, methodical process that unfolds over nearly two decades.

- ## The Rock Hammer: The Seed of an Idea

The first tool in Andy's escape plan is a small rock hammer, which he requests from his friend Ellis "Red" Redding, the prison's "man who can get things." To the untrained eye, the rock hammer appears to be a harmless tool, used by Andy to pursue his hobby of shaping rocks into small carvings. However, the rock hammer is much more than a mere hobby tool; it is the key to his eventual freedom.

Andy begins to use the rock hammer to chip away at the concrete wall of his cell, a process that takes years of painstaking effort. He works slowly and quietly, taking care to avoid drawing attention to his activities. The debris from his work is discreetly disposed of by scattering it in the prison yard during his daily walks. Andy's seemingly innocuous hobby becomes the foundation of his escape, a long-term project that requires immense patience and a keen understanding of human nature.

- ## The Tunnel: A Monument to Persistence

As the years pass, Andy's work on the tunnel continues, hidden behind a series of posters that he hangs on the wall of his cell. The first of these posters is of Rita Hayworth, followed by others, including Marilyn Monroe and Raquel Welch. These posters not only serve as a cover for the tunnel but also represent Andy's enduring connection to the outside world—a symbol of hope in a place where hope is a rare commodity.

The tunnel is a testament to Andy's perseverance and his ability to think several steps ahead. He understands that his plan will take years to come to fruition, but he is willing to invest the time and effort required. Throughout this process, Andy keeps his intentions hidden from everyone, including his closest friends, knowing that any slip-up could lead to disaster.

- **The Financial Scheme: Setting the Stage for a New Life**

While working on the tunnel, Andy also devises a plan to secure his future once he escapes from Shawshank. Using his expertise in finance, he creates a false identity for a man named Randall Stephens, complete with forged documents and a bank account. Through this identity, Andy funnels the money he helps the warden launder, effectively building a nest egg for his life after prison.

This financial scheme is another example of Andy's foresight and resourcefulness. He knows that escaping from Shawshank is only the first step; to truly achieve freedom, he must also have the means to start a new life far away from the prison. The creation of Randall Stephens is a masterstroke, allowing Andy to walk away from Shawshank with both his freedom and a substantial sum of money.

The Execution: The Night of the Great Escape

The culmination of Andy's years of planning comes on a stormy night in 1966, when he finally puts his escape plan into action. The execution of the plan is as meticulous as the preparation, with every detail carefully considered to maximize his chances of success.

- **The Final Preparations: A Calculated Gamble**

In the days leading up to his escape, Andy carefully positions himself for the final phase of his plan. He gathers the necessary supplies, including the false documents and cash associated with Randall Stephens. Andy's calm demeanor during this time belies the intensity of his emotions, as he prepares to take the biggest gamble of his life.

On the night of the escape, Andy acts with a precision that reflects the years of planning that have led to this moment. He uses the rock hammer to remove the last section of the tunnel, crawling through the narrow passage he has painstakingly carved over the years. The tunnel leads to a sewage pipe, which Andy breaks open, allowing him to crawl through the filth to freedom. The choice of the sewage pipe is both practical and symbolic, representing the final indignity Andy must endure before he can reclaim his life.

- **The Journey Through the Sewage: The Final Trial**

The journey through the sewage pipe is the most harrowing part of Andy's escape. The pipe, filled with the foulest of waste, stretches for hundreds of yards and requires Andy to summon every ounce of his physical and mental strength to push through. This moment is often seen as a powerful metaphor for the lengths to which Andy is willing to go to achieve his freedom—a journey through the lowest depths of human existence, emerging cleansed on the other side.

Andy's emergence from the sewage pipe, into the clean rain of the outside world, is one of the most iconic moments in the story. Standing in the downpour, arms outstretched, Andy experiences a moment of pure liberation—a moment that has been years in the making. It is a triumphant culmination of his journey, both physical and emotional, from a wrongfully convicted man to a free individual who has outwitted the system that sought to destroy him.

- **The Final Steps: Outwitting the System**

After escaping from Shawshank, Andy puts the final part of his plan into motion. He dons civilian clothes he had previously hidden near the exit point and makes his way to the nearest town. There, he withdraws the money under the Randall Stephens alias, effectively securing his financial future. Andy then sends evidence of the warden's corruption to a local newspaper, ensuring that justice is served, even as he disappears into the shadows.

Warden Norton, upon realizing what has happened, is faced with the collapse of his empire. The discovery of Andy's empty cell, the open tunnel, and the incriminating evidence sent to the authorities leaves Norton with no escape. In a final act of desperation, he takes his own life, unable to face the consequences of his actions.

Andy, meanwhile, makes his way to the Mexican coastal town of Zihuatanejo, a place he had long dreamed of during his time at Shawshank. There, he begins a new life, free from the constraints of his past and the oppression of the prison. The escape from Shawshank is complete, not just in the physical sense, but in the total reinvention of Andy Dufresne's life.

The Themes: Hope, Redemption, and the Human Spirit

The escape from Shawshank is more than just a thrilling story of a prison break; it is a profound exploration of hope, redemption, and the resilience of the human spirit. Throughout his years at Shawshank, Andy Dufresne embodies the idea that hope is a powerful force, capable of sustaining a person even in the darkest of times. His quiet determination and refusal to let Shawshank break him serve as an inspiration to others, particularly Red, who initially dismisses hope as dangerous but ultimately comes to embrace it as a vital part of his own journey.

Andy's escape is also a story of redemption—not just for himself, but for the other inmates who come to see him as a symbol of something greater than the bleakness of their existence. Through his actions, Andy redeems not only his own life but also the lives of those around him, offering them a glimpse of a world beyond the prison walls.

The story of Andy Dufresne's escape from Shawshank has resonated with audiences for decades because it speaks to the universal desire for freedom and the belief that, no matter how dire the circumstances, there is always a way to overcome them. The escape from Shawshank is a testament to the power of hope, the strength of the human spirit, and the idea that true freedom is worth any sacrifice.

The Legacy: A Timeless Tale of Triumph

The legacy of the Shawshank escape is one that has endured for generations. Both the novella and the film adaptation have become cultural touchstones, celebrated for their powerful storytelling and unforgettable characters. Andy Dufresne's journey from prisoner to free man is a story that continues to inspire, reminding us that even in the darkest of places, there is always the possibility of light.

The escape from Shawshank has also become a symbol of resilience and the belief that, with enough determination and cunning, even the most insurmountable obstacles can be overcome. It is a story that has been retold, referenced, and revered in countless ways, each time reaffirming its status as one of the greatest tales of escape ever conceived.

In conclusion, the escape from Shawshank is not just a fictional account of a prison break; it is a narrative that transcends its setting, offering profound insights into the nature of hope, the quest for redemption, and the enduring strength of the human spirit. It is a story that will continue to captivate and inspire for generations to come.

Chapter 33: Billy Hayes

The tale of Billy Hayes is one of the most gripping and harrowing stories of imprisonment and escape in the 20th century. His journey, which began with a youthful mistake and spiraled into a nightmare of incarceration in a foreign land, culminated in a daring escape that captured the world's imagination. Immortalized in the book *Midnight Express* and its subsequent film adaptation, Hayes' story is a powerful narrative of survival, desperation, and the indomitable will to regain freedom.

Background: A Fateful Decision

Billy Hayes was born on April 3, 1947, in New York City, growing up in a middle-class family. His life took a dramatic turn when, in his early twenties, he decided to smuggle hashish from Turkey to the United States. Like many young people of the era, Hayes was drawn to the counterculture movement of the 1960s and early 1970s, which often involved experimentation with drugs. For Hayes, this experiment took the form of smuggling small amounts of hashish, which he had successfully done several times before.

In 1970, however, things went disastrously wrong. On October 7, 1970, as Hayes was about to board a plane back to the United States from Istanbul, Turkish authorities caught him with two kilograms of hashish strapped to his body. This marked the beginning of a terrifying ordeal that would last nearly five years.

Incarceration: Life in a Turkish Prison

Upon his arrest, Billy Hayes was taken to a Turkish police station, where he was interrogated and subjected to harsh treatment. The Turkish legal system, known for its severe punishment of drug offenses, showed no mercy to Hayes. Initially sentenced to four years and two months in prison, his sentence was later extended to 30 years following a retrial, which left him devastated.

Hayes was sent to Sağmalcılar Prison in Istanbul, a facility notorious for its brutal conditions. The prison was overcrowded, unsanitary, and violent, with frequent outbreaks of disease and gang-related conflicts among the inmates. The guards were often corrupt and abusive, exploiting prisoners for their own gain. The environment was one of constant fear and tension, where survival depended on forming alliances and avoiding the wrath of both guards and fellow inmates.

Hayes, a young American far from home, found himself in an alien and hostile world. He had to navigate the dangerous prison culture, learning the rules and unwritten codes that governed daily life in Sağmalcılar. Over time, he developed a network of friends and allies, including other foreigners and sympathetic Turkish inmates, who helped him endure the harsh realities of prison life.

The psychological toll of incarceration was immense. Hayes struggled with the isolation from his family and friends, the uncertainty of his future, and the constant threat of violence. He kept himself sane by maintaining a strict routine, exercising, studying languages, and writing letters to his family. Despite the bleakness of his situation, Hayes never gave up hope of finding a way out.

The Desperation to Escape

As the years passed and the reality of his extended sentence set in, Billy Hayes became increasingly desperate to escape. The thought of spending decades in the brutal environment of a Turkish prison was unbearable, and he knew that his only chance of regaining his freedom was to take matters into his own hands.

Hayes made several attempts to escape, each one more dangerous and risky than the last. His first plan involved bribing a guard to smuggle him out of the prison, but it fell apart when the guard was arrested before the plan could be executed. Another plan involved disguising himself as a woman and slipping out of the prison during visiting hours, but this too was foiled by the strict security measures in place.

Despite these setbacks, Hayes remained determined. He spent hours studying the layout of the prison, observing the routines of the guards, and searching for any weakness in the security system. He also made contact with other inmates who had experience with escape attempts, learning from their successes and failures.

In the meantime, conditions in the prison continued to deteriorate. The overcrowding worsened, and violence between inmates became more frequent and more brutal. Hayes witnessed horrific acts of violence and cruelty, which only strengthened his resolve to escape.

The Final Plan: A Daring Escape

In 1975, after nearly five years of imprisonment, Billy Hayes finally saw an opportunity to escape. By this time, he had been transferred to İmralı Prison, an island facility in the Sea of Marmara, where security was less stringent than in Sağmalcılar. The island's isolation was both a blessing and a curse; while it was difficult to escape from, the guards were less vigilant, and the terrain offered potential hiding places.

Hayes carefully planned his escape, taking into account the geography of the island, the routines of the guards, and the availability of resources. He knew that the window of opportunity would be small and that he would have to act quickly and decisively.

On October 2, 1975, Hayes made his move. Under the cover of night, he slipped away from his work detail and headed for the shoreline. He knew that the island was surrounded by dangerous waters, but he was prepared to take the risk. Hayes had studied the tides and currents, and he believed that he could swim to freedom.

After reaching the shore, Hayes stripped off his clothes and plunged into the cold, choppy waters of the Sea of Marmara. The swim was grueling, and he was nearly swept away by the strong currents, but he managed to keep his bearings and continued to push forward. After several hours of swimming, he reached the mainland, exhausted but alive.

Once on the mainland, Hayes knew he had to act quickly to avoid recapture. He stole a rowboat and rowed along the coast until he reached a small village, where he was able to blend in with the local population. From there, he made his way to Istanbul, avoiding police checkpoints and relying on the help of sympathetic locals who provided him with food, clothing, and shelter.

Finally, after several days of evading capture, Billy Hayes crossed the border into Greece, where he sought refuge at the U.S. embassy. He was eventually flown back to the United States, where he was reunited with his family and friends.

The Aftermath: A Story That Captured the World's Imagination

Billy Hayes' escape from İmralı Prison made headlines around the world. His story was seen as a triumph of the human spirit, a tale of resilience, courage, and the desire for freedom. However, it also sparked controversy, particularly in Turkey, where the government was outraged by Hayes' portrayal of Turkish prisons and sought to downplay the severity of his experiences.

In 1977, Hayes published his memoir, *Midnight Express*, which detailed his experiences in Turkish prisons and his dramatic escape. The book became an international bestseller and was later adapted into a film of the same name, directed by Alan Parker and written by Oliver Stone. The film, released in 1978, was a critical and commercial success, but it also drew criticism for its depiction of Turkey and its people, which many felt was unfair and biased.

Hayes himself acknowledged that the film took creative liberties with his story, exaggerating certain aspects for dramatic effect. He expressed regret that the film's portrayal of Turkey had caused offense and stated that his intention was never to vilify the Turkish people but to shed light on the harsh realities of the prison system.

Despite the controversy, *Midnight Express* remains one of the most iconic prison escape stories of all time. Billy Hayes' journey from youthful recklessness to hardened prisoner and finally to freedom is a powerful narrative that resonates with audiences around the world.

The Legacy: A Story of Survival and Redemption

Billy Hayes' story is more than just a tale of escape; it is a story of survival and redemption. His experiences in Turkish prisons forced him to confront the darkest aspects of human nature, both in others and within himself. The brutal conditions, the violence, and the isolation tested his physical and mental limits, but they also taught him valuable lessons about resilience, courage, and the importance of hope.

Hayes' escape from İmralı Prison is a testament to the power of the human spirit to overcome even the most daunting obstacles. His determination to regain his freedom, despite the overwhelming odds against him, is an inspiration to anyone who has ever faced adversity.

In the years following his escape, Hayes has continued to share his story with audiences around the world, speaking about his experiences and the lessons he learned from them. He has also worked to raise awareness about the conditions in prisons and the need for reform, drawing on his own experiences to advocate for change.

The legacy of Billy Hayes' escape is one of resilience, courage, and the enduring desire for freedom. His story serves as a reminder that, no matter how dire the circumstances, there is always hope for a better future. It is a story that continues to inspire and captivate, proving that the human spirit can triumph even in the face of the most overwhelming challenges.

Chapter 34: Escape from HMP Pentridge

The escape from Her Majesty's Prison Pentridge, commonly known as HMP Pentridge, stands as one of the most audacious and dramatic prison breaks in Australian history. Located in Coburg, Victoria, Pentridge Prison was once one of the most secure and infamous penal institutions in Australia. Over its long history, the prison housed some of the country's most dangerous criminals, yet it was also the site of a daring and highly organized escape that shook the foundations of the Australian penal system.

The History of HMP Pentridge

Before delving into the details of the escape, it's essential to understand the history and significance of HMP Pentridge. The prison was established in 1851, initially serving as a temporary holding facility during the Victorian Gold Rush, a time when the population of Melbourne swelled dramatically due to the influx of prospectors. The prison quickly expanded and became a permanent institution, designed to accommodate the growing number of criminals in the colony.

Pentridge Prison was constructed as a maximum-security facility, with various divisions and blocks built to house different categories of prisoners. Over the years, it became known for its harsh conditions, with inmates subjected to long hours of hard labor, strict discipline, and solitary confinement. The prison's bluestone walls, which were over 16 feet high and topped with barbed wire, made it nearly impossible to escape.

The prison also became notorious for its role in carrying out executions, with dedicated gallows where more than 11 men were hanged between 1951 and 1967. Pentridge was closed in 1997, and the site has since been redeveloped, but its legacy as a place of punishment and containment remains a significant part of Australian history.

The Criminals Behind the Escape

The escape from HMP Pentridge involved three men: Ronald Ryan, Peter Walker, and William "Slim" Halliday. Each of these men had a notorious criminal background, and their desperation to escape from Pentridge stemmed from the harsh conditions they faced and the long sentences they were serving.

- **Ronald Ryan** was the central figure in the escape. Born in Melbourne in 1925, Ryan had a troubled childhood marked by poverty and neglect. He turned to crime at an early age, and by the time he was in his twenties, he had accumulated a lengthy criminal record, including convictions for burglary and armed robbery. In 1964, Ryan was sentenced to 10 years in Pentridge Prison for armed robbery. However, in 1965, he and fellow inmate Peter Walker hatched a plan to escape.
- **Peter Walker**, born in 1941, was also a career criminal. He had a history of violent crimes, including armed robbery and assault, and was serving a lengthy sentence at Pentridge. Walker was known for his cunning and resourcefulness, qualities that would prove invaluable during the escape.
- **William "Slim" Halliday**, though not directly involved in the Ryan-Walker escape, is often associated with Pentridge's history of prison breaks. Halliday was known as "The Houdini of Boggo Road," famous for his multiple escape attempts from prisons across Australia, including Pentridge. His legacy as an escape artist served as inspiration for other inmates, including Ryan and Walker.

The Planning of the Escape

The escape from HMP Pentridge was not a spur-of-the-moment decision but rather a carefully planned operation that took months of preparation. Ryan and Walker knew that escaping from Pentridge would be no easy feat. The prison's security measures were stringent, and the guards were vigilant. However, the two men were determined to break free.

The planning began with meticulous observation of the prison's routines and security weaknesses. Ryan and Walker studied the daily schedules of the guards, noting the times when they were most vulnerable. They also paid close attention to the physical layout of the prison, looking for potential escape routes.

One of the key factors in the escape plan was the acquisition of a firearm. Ryan and Walker knew that they would need a weapon to overpower the guards and facilitate their escape. Through contacts on the outside, they managed to smuggle a rifle into the prison, hiding it in a place where they could easily access it during the escape.

The escape plan hinged on timing and coordination. Ryan and Walker knew that they would need to move quickly and decisively once they made their move. They planned to escape during a routine exercise period when the guards were slightly more relaxed. The plan also involved taking a prison officer hostage to use as leverage during the escape.

The Escape: A Desperate Bid for Freedom

The escape attempt took place on December 19, 1965. The day began like any other at Pentridge, with the prisoners going about their daily routines. Ryan and Walker had carefully chosen this day, knowing that the guards would be slightly less vigilant due to the upcoming holiday season.

As planned, the two men made their move during the exercise period. Armed with the smuggled rifle, they approached one of the guards, forcing him to hand over his keys. With the keys in hand, they unlocked a gate leading to the prison yard. From there, they made their way to the outer perimeter of the prison.

At the outer gate, Ryan and Walker encountered a group of prison officers. In the ensuing confrontation, Ryan fired the rifle, killing a prison officer named George Hodson. The killing of Hodson marked a tragic and pivotal moment in the escape, as it turned what might have been a relatively routine breakout into a deadly confrontation.

Despite the chaos, Ryan and Walker managed to escape from the prison grounds, fleeing into the streets of Melbourne. Their escape sparked a massive manhunt, with police and prison authorities mobilizing all available resources to track down the fugitives. The killing of George Hodson also intensified the urgency of the manhunt, as the authorities were now dealing with dangerous, armed criminals who had already proven their willingness to kill.

The Manhunt: A Nation on Edge

The escape of Ronald Ryan and Peter Walker from HMP Pentridge sent shockwaves throughout Australia. The public was gripped by fear and anxiety, as the fugitives were considered extremely dangerous. The authorities launched one of the largest manhunts in Australian history, with hundreds of police officers, including special units, combing the streets of Melbourne and the surrounding areas in search of the escapees.

The media played a significant role in the manhunt, with newspapers, radio, and television providing constant updates on the progress of the search. The public was urged to remain vigilant and report any sightings of the fugitives. The intense media coverage and public interest in the case added to the pressure on the authorities to capture Ryan and Walker quickly.

Ryan and Walker, meanwhile, were on the run, desperately trying to evade capture. They moved from one hiding place to another, relying on the help of criminal associates and sympathizers who provided them with food, shelter, and transportation. Despite their efforts to stay hidden, the net was slowly closing in on them.

After several days on the run, Ryan and Walker decided to split up, hoping that separating would increase their chances of evading capture. Ryan made his way to Sydney, while Walker remained in Victoria. Both men continued to move from place to place, but their options were rapidly dwindling as the authorities closed in.

Capture and Aftermath: The End of the Road

The manhunt came to a dramatic end in late December 1965. Peter Walker was the first to be captured, apprehended by police in Victoria. His capture was a significant breakthrough for the authorities, as it allowed them to focus all their efforts on finding Ryan.

Ronald Ryan, however, remained at large for a few more days. He was finally captured in Sydney on December 30, 1965, after being cornered by police in a boarding house. His capture marked the end of one of the most intense manhunts in Australian history.

The aftermath of the escape was significant, both for Ryan and Walker and for the Australian penal system as a whole. Ronald Ryan was charged with the murder of George Hodson, and his trial became one of the most high-profile criminal cases in Australian history. Despite his defense team's efforts to argue that the shooting was accidental, Ryan was convicted of murder and sentenced to death.

Peter Walker, meanwhile, was sentenced to a lengthy prison term for his role in the escape and for his previous crimes. He would spend many more years behind bars before eventually being released on parole.

The Execution of Ronald Ryan: A Controversial End

Ronald Ryan's conviction and death sentence sparked a heated debate in Australia about the use of the death penalty. At the time, capital punishment was still legal in Victoria, but there was growing public opposition to its use. Ryan's case became a focal point for the anti-death penalty movement, with many people arguing that his execution would be a miscarriage of justice.

Despite the public outcry and appeals for clemency, the Victorian government decided to proceed with Ryan's execution. On February 3, 1967, Ronald Ryan was hanged at Pentridge Prison, making him the last person to be executed in Australia.

Ryan's execution marked the end of an era in Australian legal history, as it was the final use of the death penalty in the country. In the years that followed, capital punishment was abolished in all Australian states and territories, and Ryan's case became a symbol of the movement to end the death penalty.

The Legacy of the Pentridge Escape

The escape from HMP Pentridge remains one of the most famous and dramatic prison breaks in Australian history. The daring nature of the escape, the tragic death of George Hodson, and the subsequent manhunt and trial of Ronald Ryan all contributed to the case's notoriety.

The escape also had a lasting impact on the Australian penal system. In the wake of the escape, prison security measures were reviewed and tightened, with a particular focus on preventing future breakouts. The case also highlighted the harsh conditions in Australian prisons, leading to calls for reform and improvements in the treatment of inmates.

For many Australians, the escape from Pentridge is remembered as a cautionary tale about the dangers of a life of crime and the consequences of attempting to defy the law. Ronald Ryan and Peter Walker's desperate bid for freedom ultimately ended in tragedy, with one man dead and another facing the ultimate punishment.

Today, the story of the Pentridge escape continues to be a source of fascination and intrigue, serving as a reminder of a turbulent time in Australia's criminal justice history. The legacy of the escape lives on in the collective memory of the nation, a symbol of both the brutality of the past and the enduring desire for freedom that drives even the most desperate of men.

Chapter 35: Escape from Dannemora

The "Escape from Dannemora," also known as the Clinton Correctional Facility escape, is one of the most infamous prison breaks in recent American history. This dramatic event captivated the nation, leading to a massive manhunt and a series of investigations into the circumstances that allowed two convicted murderers to break free from a maximum-security prison. The escape from Dannemora is a story of ingenuity, manipulation, betrayal, and the failure of a system designed to contain the most dangerous criminals.

The Clinton Correctional Facility: A Fortress in the North

Clinton Correctional Facility, located in Dannemora, New York, is one of the oldest and most secure prisons in the United States. Established in 1845, it was designed to house the state's most hardened and dangerous criminals. Nicknamed "Little Siberia" due to its remote location and harsh climate, Clinton Correctional Facility was considered nearly escape-proof. The prison is surrounded by towering walls, razor wire, and numerous guard towers, with strict protocols in place to prevent any inmate from escaping.

Despite its reputation as a fortress, Clinton Correctional Facility had seen its share of violence and unrest over the years. Inmates at Dannemora were often serving long sentences for serious crimes, creating a tense and volatile environment. The prison's harsh conditions, including overcrowding, poor living conditions, and the isolation of being so far from civilization, added to the stress and desperation felt by many inmates. Yet, for all its difficulties, few could have imagined that an escape would take place from within its walls, especially not one as meticulously planned and executed as the escape in June 2015.

The Escapees: Richard Matt and David Sweat

The two men at the center of the escape from Dannemora were Richard Matt and David Sweat, both serving lengthy sentences for violent crimes. Richard Matt, born in 1966, was a career criminal with a long history of violent behavior. He had been convicted of murder in 1997 after kidnapping, torturing, and killing his former boss, William Rickerson. Known for his cunning and ruthlessness, Matt had a reputation as a manipulative and dangerous inmate.

David Sweat, born in 1980, was serving a life sentence without the possibility of parole for the 2002 murder of Broome County Sheriff's Deputy Kevin Tarsia. Sweat and his accomplices had ambushed Tarsia during a robbery, shooting him multiple times before running him over with a car. Sweat was younger than Matt but equally determined to escape the confines of prison. The two men formed a close bond while serving time at Clinton Correctional Facility, sharing a common desire to regain their freedom at any cost.

The Plan: A Plot Months in the Making

The escape from Dannemora was not a spontaneous act but the result of months of careful planning and preparation. Richard Matt and David Sweat were methodical in their approach, using their time in prison to gather the tools and information they needed to break free. Their plan involved a combination of ingenuity, manipulation of prison staff, and exploiting the weaknesses in the prison's security system.

The first step in their plan was to gain access to the areas of the prison that would allow them to escape. Matt and Sweat both worked as laborers in the prison's tailor shop, where they sewed uniforms for state employees. This job provided them with a level of freedom not afforded to other inmates, as well as access to tools and materials that could be used in their escape.

Over time, Matt and Sweat began to stockpile tools, including hacksaw blades, chisels, and other implements that could be used to cut through metal and concrete. They were able to obtain these items with the help of a civilian employee, Joyce Mitchell, who worked as a supervisor in the prison's tailor shop. Mitchell, who had developed relationships with both inmates, was manipulated into smuggling the tools into the prison and providing other assistance in their escape plan.

Matt and Sweat's plan involved cutting through the walls of their cells and accessing the network of tunnels and pipes beneath the prison. They spent weeks meticulously cutting through the steel walls of their cells, careful to make only a little progress each night to avoid detection. Once they had cut through the walls, they crawled through the narrow tunnels, eventually reaching an outside wall of the prison. There, they cut a hole in the wall and made their way to a manhole cover outside the prison's perimeter.

The Role of Joyce Mitchell: The Inside Accomplice

Joyce Mitchell's involvement in the escape from Dannemora was one of the most shocking aspects of the case. A middle-aged wife and mother, Mitchell seemed an unlikely accomplice in a prison break. However, her relationship with Richard Matt and David Sweat had developed over time, leading her to become deeply entangled in their plot.

Mitchell had worked at Clinton Correctional Facility for several years, where she was responsible for overseeing inmates in the tailor shop. During this time, she became close to both Matt and Sweat, who were charismatic and manipulative. Matt, in particular, used his charm to seduce and manipulate Mitchell, convincing her that he cared for her and that they could have a future together outside of prison.

Mitchell's relationship with the two inmates became increasingly inappropriate, with reports suggesting that she engaged in sexual relationships with both men. She was also persuaded to smuggle tools and other contraband into the prison, believing that she was helping the men she had grown close to. Mitchell's actions would ultimately play a crucial role in the success of the escape.

In addition to smuggling tools, Mitchell was supposed to assist Matt and Sweat by providing them with a getaway car after they escaped from the prison. The plan called for her to meet the two men at a designated location near the prison and drive them to a safe house. However, on the night of the escape, Mitchell had a change of heart and did not show up, leaving Matt and Sweat to fend for themselves once they were outside the prison.

The Escape: A Daring Breakout

On the night of June 5, 2015, Richard Matt and David Sweat put their escape plan into action. After months of preparation, they were finally ready to break free from Clinton Correctional Facility. The two men crawled through the holes they had cut in the walls of their cells, entered the prison's underground tunnels, and made their way to the outside wall.

The escape itself was a feat of engineering and determination. Matt and Sweat crawled through a maze of pipes and tunnels, squeezing through tight spaces and cutting through obstacles as they went. They used a hacksaw blade to cut through a steel pipe and crawled for nearly an hour through a series of underground tunnels. Finally, they reached a steam pipe that led to a manhole cover outside the prison walls.

In the early hours of June 6, 2015, Matt and Sweat emerged from the manhole cover, just 500 feet from the prison's perimeter. They had successfully escaped from one of the most secure prisons in the country, an act that would have seemed impossible to many. However, their escape was only the beginning of a much larger ordeal.

The Manhunt: A Massive Search Operation

The discovery of the escape sparked one of the largest manhunts in New York State history. When prison officials realized that Matt and Sweat were missing, they immediately launched a search of the prison and its surrounding areas. However, the two men had a significant head start, having escaped hours before their absence was discovered.

The manhunt for Matt and Sweat involved multiple law enforcement agencies, including the New York State Police, the FBI, the U.S. Marshals Service, and other local and federal agencies. Thousands of law enforcement officers were deployed to search the dense forests and rural areas surrounding Dannemora, where the men were believed to be hiding.

The search was complicated by the rugged terrain and the fact that Matt and Sweat were experienced outdoorsmen who knew how to survive in the wilderness. The two men had also prepared for their escape by gathering supplies, including food, clothing, and camping gear, which they carried with them as they fled.

The manhunt lasted for more than three weeks, during which time the public and the media closely followed the developments. The search area was expanded as law enforcement received tips and sightings of the two escapees. However, the dense forests and rural landscape made it difficult to track the men down, and the authorities were frustrated by the lack of progress.

The Capture of Richard Matt: A Violent End

The manhunt for Richard Matt and David Sweat came to a violent end on June 26, 2015, when Matt was shot and killed by law enforcement officers. Matt had been spotted by a homeowner in the town of Malone, New York, about 40 miles from the prison. The homeowner reported seeing Matt near his cabin, leading to a response from law enforcement.

A team of officers, including members of the U.S. Customs and Border Protection's Tactical Unit, surrounded the area where Matt was hiding. When they confronted him, Matt refused to surrender and was shot and killed by the officers. It was later revealed that Matt was armed with a shotgun, which he had stolen from a hunting cabin.

The death of Richard Matt marked the end of the manhunt for one of the two escapees, but the search for David Sweat continued. Matt's death was seen as a significant development in the case, but authorities were still determined to capture Sweat alive.

The Capture of David Sweat: The End of the Manhunt

Two days after Richard Matt was killed, David Sweat was captured by law enforcement officers. On June 28, 2015, Sweat was spotted by a New York State Trooper in the town of Constable, New York, just a few miles from the Canadian border. The trooper, Sgt. Jay Cook, was on patrol when he noticed a man walking along a rural road who matched Sweat's description.

When Cook approached Sweat, the fugitive attempted to flee, leading the trooper to give chase. Cook eventually shot Sweat twice in the torso, incapacitating him and allowing him to be taken into custody. Sweat was then airlifted to Albany Medical Center, where he was treated for his injuries.

The capture of David Sweat brought an end to the nearly month-long manhunt that had gripped the nation. Sweat's capture was met with relief by law enforcement and the public, who had been on edge during the weeks of uncertainty. With both escapees now accounted for, attention turned to the investigation into how the escape had been possible.

The Aftermath: Investigations and Consequences

In the wake of the escape, there was intense scrutiny of Clinton Correctional Facility and the circumstances that had allowed Richard Matt and David Sweat to break free. The New York State Inspector General launched an investigation into the escape, focusing on the prison's security procedures, the actions of the prison staff, and the role of Joyce Mitchell in aiding the escape.

The investigation revealed a series of failures and lapses in security at Clinton Correctional Facility. These included inadequate supervision of inmates, lax enforcement of prison rules, and a culture of complacency among the staff. The investigation also found that several prison employees had failed to follow proper procedures, allowing Matt and Sweat to carry out their plan without detection.

As a result of the investigation, several prison employees were disciplined or fired, including the superintendent of Clinton Correctional Facility. Joyce Mitchell was arrested and charged with promoting prison contraband and facilitating the escape. In September 2015, she pleaded guilty to the charges and was sentenced to 2 1/3 to 7 years in prison.

The escape from Dannemora also led to changes in prison policies and procedures across New York State. Governor Andrew Cuomo ordered a comprehensive review of the state's prison system, resulting in new measures to improve security and prevent future escapes. These included increased surveillance of inmates, stricter controls on tools and materials, and enhanced training for prison staff.

The Legacy of the Escape: A Cautionary Tale

The escape from Dannemora remains one of the most dramatic and well-publicized prison breaks in modern American history. The story of Richard Matt and David Sweat's escape, the massive manhunt that followed, and the investigations that ensued captivated the nation and raised important questions about prison security and the criminal justice system.

The escape serves as a cautionary tale about the potential for even the most secure prisons to be compromised by determined and resourceful inmates. It also highlights the importance of vigilance, accountability, and the need for continuous improvement in the management of correctional facilities.

For the residents of Dannemora and the surrounding areas, the escape was a traumatic and unsettling experience, one that exposed the vulnerabilities of a system designed to protect the public from dangerous criminals. The event left a lasting impact on the community and served as a reminder of the potential for violence and chaos when the control of dangerous individuals is lost.

In popular culture, the escape from Dannemora was dramatized in the 2018 television miniseries "Escape at Dannemora," directed by Ben Stiller and starring Benicio del Toro, Paul Dano, and Patricia Arquette. The series brought renewed attention to the case and provided a detailed, though dramatized, account of the events leading up to and following the escape.

Ultimately, the escape from Dannemora is a story of human ingenuity, the consequences of poor oversight, and the lengths to which some individuals will go to regain their freedom. It is a story that will be remembered for years to come as a testament to the challenges and complexities of managing a maximum-security prison in the modern era.

Epilogue

As we come to the end of our journey through the gripping narratives of "True Stories of Prison Escapes," we reflect on the resilience, ingenuity, and sheer determination displayed by those who dared to defy the confines of captivity. From the daring exploits of inmates like Frank Abagnale Jr. and Henri Charrière to the audacious breakouts from Alcatraz and Shawshank, each tale has offered a glimpse into the indomitable human spirit's quest for freedom.

But beyond the adrenaline-fueled escapes and dramatic showdowns with authority lies a deeper truth—a truth that transcends the boundaries of time and circumstance. It is the truth that resilience knows no bounds, that hope can flourish even in the darkest of places, and that the human spirit is capable of extraordinary feats when faced with adversity.

Through these stories, we have witnessed the triumph of the human will over seemingly insurmountable odds. We have seen ordinary individuals rise to meet extraordinary challenges, drawing upon reserves of courage and resourcefulness they never knew they possessed. And we have been reminded that, in the face of injustice and oppression, the pursuit of freedom is a fundamental human right—one worth fighting for, no matter the cost.

As we bid farewell to the characters who have shared their stories with us, let us carry their legacy forward in our hearts and minds. Let us remember their courage, their resilience, and their unwavering determination to reclaim their liberty. And let us be inspired by their example to never lose sight of our own dreams and aspirations, no matter the obstacles we may face along the way.

For in the end, "True Stories of Prison Escapes" is not just a collection of tales—it is a testament to the enduring power of the human spirit to overcome adversity and forge a path to freedom, no matter the odds. And as we turn the final page, may we carry with us the lessons learned and the stories shared, knowing that the pursuit of liberty is a journey worth embarking upon, time and time again.

The End.